Charlie Wetzel
and Stephanie Wetzel

HarperCollins
LEADERSHIP
An Imprint of HarperCollins

THE MARVEL STUDIOS STORY

How a Failing Comic Book Publisher
Became a Hollywood Superhero

Published by HarperCollins Leadership, an imprint of HarperCollins Focus LLC.

Published in association with Yates & Yates: https://www.yates2.com/.

Book design by Aubrey Khan, Neuwirth & Associates.

ISBN 978-1-4002-1619-2 (eBook)
ISBN 978-1-4002-1613-0 (HC)

Library of Congress Control Number: 2020931802

Printed in the United States of America
20 21 22 23 LSC 10 9 8 7 6 5 4 3 2 1

CONTENTS

1939
Frank Torpey convinces Martin Goodman to publish a comic book, resulting in Marvel Comics #1.

1941
Stan Lee becomes editor in chief of Timely Comics.

1944
Captain America appears in a movie serial created by Republic Pictures.

1972
Lee becomes president and publisher, handing over editor in chief duties to Roy Thomas.

1961
Goodman asks Lee to create a group of superheroes, so Lee and Jack Kirby create the Fantastic Four.

1974
Lee steps down as president of Marvel but remains publisher.

1981
Marvel Productions sets up in Los Angeles.

1986
The Marvel Entertainment Group is established.

1991
Marvel goes public selling stock in an IPO.

1993
Marvel Films is founded with Avi Arad as CEO and President.

2019
Disney acquires 21st Century Fox.

2015
Disney reorganizes Marvel.

2012
Marvel films start being distributed by Disney (from 2008–2011 Marvel Films were distributed by Paramount Pictures).

2009
Disney acquires Marvel Entertainment for $4.24 billion.

2006
Arad steps down as chairman and CEO of Marvel Studio and as chief creative officer of Marvel Entertainment.

2002
Lee sues Marvel Enterprises and Marvel Characters for $10 million.

2005
Marvel re-obtains rights to Iron Man.

1998
Marvel is delisted on NYSE.

1996
The Marvel group of companies files for bankruptcy.

1995
Marvel posts an annual loss.

"I'm just a
kid from Brooklyn."

—CAPTAIN AMERICA

INTRODUCTION

To fully understand the success story of Marvel Studios, where should we start? Most people think of Stan Lee, the quirky old man who made cameo appearances in every Marvel Studios film up through *Avengers: Endgame.* Movie fans mourned the news of his death in 2018 at the age of ninety-five. Movie and comic book fans know he was more than just a loquacious old man; he was an inseparable part of Marvel for nearly eighty years.

Others might want to start the story with the founding of Marvel Productions in 1981, though that was really a non-event that made no significant impact on Hollywood.

How about starting with *Iron Man,* Marvel Studios' first movie made in 2008? Hardly anybody expected it to be a box office success. The concept had been kicked around in Hollywood for more than twenty years. Writers didn't want to be a part of it. The star had a rocky past. The director had never done a big superhero action film. Producers had a terrible time getting the film financed. Yet, it was a hit.

The reality is that if you really want to understand the Marvel Studios story, you need to understand Marvel Comics. And to understand Marvel Comics, you must go all the way back to how they got their start. The Marvel story starts, not with a superhero, but with a poor kid from Brooklyn in the early twentieth century, Marvel founder Martin Goodman. Much of what has made Marvel Studios and its films unique—the kinds of superheroes Marvel creates, the sheer *number* of characters in its portfolio, the way they interact in their shared universe, and the way the business evolved with the collaboration of artists and business people—was all set in motion from the very beginning. So that's where we'll begin.

Pulp Fiction before *Pulp Fiction*

Moe Goodman, who went by "Martin" most of his life, was born in 1908. His parents were from Lithuania, which was then part of the Russian Empire, and like many Jewish people during that era, they emigrated to America to seek a better life. His father, Isaac, was a tailor. His mother, Anna, raised him and his fourteen siblings.

Maybe Goodman was destined to become a publisher. According to family lore, when he was a child, he used to spend his time creating magazine mockups by cutting out stories and articles he liked and pasting them together. That was during the heyday of newspaper and magazine publishing. You couldn't walk down any street in that era without passing dozens of newsstands.

Newsstands ranged in size from tiny shacks not much bigger than a phone booth, to alcoves in the walls of a building, to long storefronts, to cigar-shop additions. Some were even sizeable stand-alone buildings with multiple open windows, where sellers stood behind narrow counters making sales. Of course, they all sold newspapers. And back in those days, a big city like New York didn't have one paper or two. It had *dozens*. In the 1920s, Brooklyn alone had five newspapers. There were papers published in the morning, papers published in the evening, and others published in Yiddish, Chinese, Japanese, and Polish. In 1900, more than 2,200 papers existed in the United States.[1]

But the big eye-catchers at the newsstands were *magazines.* They hung everywhere. The smallest stands would sell dozens of titles; the big ones could have hundreds. They plastered the walls. They hung in rows from the ceiling, creating a solid wall above the counters. They were displayed on counters and racks. Their colorful covers acted like billboards shouting to get a potential buyer's attention. And many additional magazines were sold "under the counter" since their content was deemed too risqué for open display to the public.

As Martin Goodman passed these newsstands every day on his walk to school, he would have been aware of two main magazine categories. The first were the high-end magazines such as *McClure's, Time, Harper's Weekly, Harper's Bazaar, Cosmopolitan,* and *The Saturday Evening Post.* The other kind of magazines were called *pulps.* These were cheaply produced and printed on cheap wood pulp paper, similar to newsprint. They were filled with short stories, serialized fiction, and sometimes even complete novels in genres such as westerns, horror stories, mysteries, suspense and adventure tales, and science fiction.

One thing all the pulps seemed to have in common was provocative covers. Pulp covers were usually even more colorful and attention-grabbing than those of the slick mainstream magazines. No matter what kinds of stories were inside, most covers featured either an action scene or a curvy woman, often scantily clad, in peril. In many ways, they were not unlike later comic book covers.

At their height of their popularity, more than 120 pulp titles[2] could be found every month at the 7,000 newsstands, 18,000 cigar stores, and 58,000 drugstores around the country.[3] So if you've ever wondered where movie director Quentin Tarantino got the title for his film *Pulp Fiction,* now you know.

> ❝ Pulp covers were usually even more colorful and attention-grabbing than those of the slick mainstream magazines. No matter what kinds of stories were inside, most covers featured either an action scene or a curvy woman, often scantily clad, in peril. In many ways, they were not unlike later comic book covers.

The Goodman Method of Publishing

It's said that Goodman quit school in 1924 at age sixteen to ride the rails all over the United States before he started his career. He hopped trains, slept in hobo camps, and ate beans cooked over an open fire.

"He knew every town and it helped him to know markets," said Jerry Perles, Goodman's lawyer and friend.[4] "I don't think you could mention a town to him that he didn't know about. He is knowledgeable about this country. It helped him a great deal later on in magazine circulation."[5]

When he got back home to New York City, he took a job as a file clerk in 1929 for a company involved in the publishing world: Eastern Distributing Company.[6] Following the stock market crash, Goodman kept his job and learned the publishing business. He thrived in this environment and worked his way up the ranks, all the way to circulation manager.[7] When Eastern Distributing got overextended and filed for bankruptcy in 1932, Goodman went into business with a partner, but that relationship didn't last long. In 1934, at the age of twenty-six, Goodman became the head of his own pulp publishing business: Newsstand Publications.

Though Goodman liked magazines, he didn't focus much on their contents. He didn't set out to educate, edify, or entertain. In fact, he once told an interviewer, "Fans are not interested in quality."[8] So what was his motivation? He wanted to run a business of his own, make a good living, and take care of his family. Magazines were just the product he chose. He would provide whatever people were willing to buy.

> **In fact, he once told an interviewer, "Fans are not interested in quality." So what was his motivation? He wanted to run a business of his own, make a good living, and take care of his family. Magazines were just the product he chose.**

But how did Goodman figure out what he to sell? By following trends. He watched the other magazines on newsstands that were selling well. And he constantly talked to his fellow publishers to find out what they were up to. One of his favorite strategies was to play golf with a fellow publisher. Or take a friend or rival to lunch. He would pick their brains and listen to them boast about what they were achieving. Afterward, he'd go back to his office and create a new magazine title based on the conversation. Whenever he caught wind of a bandwagon, he was lightning fast to jump on it.

For example, when Goodman observed that the Lone Ranger was popular, he created a pulp magazine called *The Masked Rider*. When Tarzan was big, he published a title called *Ka-Zar the Great*, about a boy brought up by lions (instead of apes) in the jungles of Africa. If western stories were selling, he would create a western magazine. If they were selling *really* well, he simply created more. That's how he ended up publishing nine different western pulp titles at the same time.[9] Goodman's motto could be summed up in a statement he made to *The Literary Digest* in January of 1937: "If you get a title that catches on, then add a few more, you're in for a nice profit."[10]

> **If you get a title that catches on, then add a few more, you're in for a nice profit."**

To minimize his financial risks, Goodman often created new companies, at least on paper, to publish some of his titles. He was soon the owner of Newsstand Publications, Western Fiction, Red Circle, and Manvis, among others. This practice enabled him to keep his taxes lower. And he could quickly shut down a company with failed titles, or protect himself from potential lawsuits. A probably unintended result was that for decades he never established a recognizable brand.

Goodman's attention was focused on two areas: the trends in the marketplace, which drove what he chose to publish, and the sale figures, which told him how each published title was doing. What happened during the time between the decision to publish a new title and a look at the sales figures from that title mattered very little to him. He relied on his editor to take care of everything in between. If Goodman expended creative energy on anything, it was on pushing his artists to create the most eye-catching covers for his magazines so that his titles would sell. And whenever he found out a title wasn't selling well enough, he'd tell the editor to kill it and create a new one.

Finally, a Comic Book

You may be wondering, *What about comic books? When did Goodman start publishing them?* That began in 1939. By then, he was making a good living cranking out magazine after magazine based on what he thought would sell. Just the previous year, he had published twenty-seven different pulp titles, with a total of *eighty-seven* individual issues.[11] One day Goodman got a visit from a friend named Frank Torpey, a salesman for a company called Funnies, Inc. Torpey pitched the idea that Goodman should branch out and publish a relatively new invention: a comic book.

Color comic strips had been around since the 1890s. In 1929, pulp fiction characters, such as Tarzan and Buck Rogers, crossed over and appeared in their own daily newspaper comic strips.[12] But it wasn't until 1935 that the first comic book was published, and just three years later, in 1938, comic books became popular with the introduction of Superman in *Action Comics #1*. The first comic book superhero, Superman, was a huge hit, selling every copy of its 200,000-print run.[13] The next year, Batman debuted in *Detective Comics #27*.

During their conversation, Torpey offered Goodman an easy inroad to publishing comic books—prepackaged illustrated content. Goodman could buy pre-made illustrated stories and simply publish them. Goodman decided to take up the offer, doing what he usually did: starting another company and inventing a new title for the magazine. This company was called Timely Comics, and the title of Goodman's first comic book was *Marvel Comics* (October issue). It soon appeared on the racks alongside newspapers and magazines.

> In 1938, comic books became popular with the introduction of Superman in *Action Comics #1*. The first comic book superhero, Superman, was a huge hit, selling every copy of its 200,000-print run. The next year, Batman debuted.

Included in the package Goodman received from Torpey were stories with two superheroes: Namor the Sub-Mariner—half human, half Atlantean—who possessed superhuman strength, could breathe underwater, and was able to fly; and the Human Torch, an android whose origin story included his creation and eventual evolution into a crime fighter. Also included was the Angel, a costumed detective who solved crimes, and a fourth character Goodman insisted upon: Ka-Zar from his pulps.[14] Funnies, Inc. adapted an earlier Ka-Zar pulp story and created art for it.

Goodman optimistically printed 80,000 copies of this first comic book. All of them sold very quickly. So he ordered a second print run of 800,000 dated November. Incredibly, all of those sold too![15] Goodman had stumbled onto a gold mine.

With the help of the Funnies, Inc. team, Goodman quickly put out a second issue (December), though he changed the name from *Marvel Comics* to *Marvel Mystery Comics.*

The Shift to Comic Books

Goodman was too good a businessperson to miss the potential within comic books. So he proceeded the same way he had with pulps. He convinced twenty-six-year-old artist and writer Joe Simon to leave Funnies, Inc. and become the editor of Timely Comics.[16] Simon hired an artist he'd worked with before: Jack Kirby. Timely was soon cranking out more comic books. In 1940, they published more issues of *Marvel Mystery Comics* (twelve issues) plus *Daring Mystery Comics* (six issues), *Mystic Comics* (four issues), and *The Human Torch* (two issues), and *Red Raven Comics* (one issue).

> **He convinced twenty-six-year-old artist and writer Joe Simon to leave Funnies, Inc. and become the editor of Timely Comics. Simon hired an artist he'd worked with before: Jack Kirby.**

As with the pulps, Goodman cared about two things: trends on the front end and sales figures on the back end. He wanted the artists and writers who worked for him to chase the trends and create a lot of content. If a new character or title sold, it stayed. If not, it didn't. But for the most part, Goodman stayed out of the creative process. In many ways he was the stereotypical business leader who says, "Don't tell me about the labor. Just show me the baby." He just wanted to be sure a lot of product went to market. This led to something Marvel became known and valued for many years later: the sheer volume of its intellectual property. Estimates today calculate that the Marvel catalog has grown to contain more than 7,000 major characters.[17] There are more than 60,000 if you count all the characters Marvel has ever created.[18] That's six times as many as their longtime rival DC.[19]

> **The Marvel catalog has grown to contain more than 7,000 major characters. There are more than 60,000 if you count all the characters Marvel has ever created.**

Every creative innovation that can be attributed to Marvel Comics came from the writers and artists who created the content, starting with Funnies, Inc. employees Carl Burgos and Bill Everett, who created the Torch and Namor the Sub-Mariner. These two initial superhero characters from Timely possessed characteristics that became trademarks of later Marvel heroes, and which made them different from the original prototypical superhero, Superman. Where Superman was always noble and seemed perfect, the Human Torch and Namor were flawed. The Human Torch was at first destructive because of his inexperience with the world. Namor was short-tempered and had a bad attitude. Many of Marvel's later superheroes would also be flawed and conflicted—with even more complexity.

Another feature that would become a trademark of later Marvel comic books and movies was introduced during the first year of Timely comic books. In *Marvel Mystery Comics #8* (June), on shelves in early 1940, the characters of Namor and the Human Torch appeared together in the same story. That might not seem like a big deal today, but in the world of comic books at the time, it was. As a matter of comparison, Batman and Superman, the two star characters for Marvel's chief rival, DC Comics, would not appear together in the same story until 1952—a dozen years later.[20]

As Big as Superman

There was only one other thing Timely Comics lacked, and that was a character of the caliber of Superman. Joe Simon and Jack Kirby took care of that problem in late 1940. Simon sent Goodman a sketch of a new superhero he and Kirby had been working on named Captain America. This character caught Goodman's attention right away. Based on his trend-watching instincts, he believed Captain America could be exciting enough to compete with Superman. Immediately, Goodman made an offer to buy the rights to the character, his standard practice. But this time, Simon and Kirby resisted. They wanted to negotiate. In the end, they accepted a royalty deal from Goodman promising them 25 percent of profits earned from the use of the character, in addition to their regular page rate.[21] As soon as the deal was made, Goodman gave the go-ahead to create a new comic book title. This one would be called *Captain America Comics*, and it went into production.

It showed up on newsstands in December 1940, with a March (1941) date on the cover. Why March? This was how the pulp magazine and comic book industries worked. The date on the cover wasn't supposed to represent when an issue *appeared* on newsstands. Instead, it indicated when the title should be *removed* from newsstands, typically about three months after arriving there.[22]

Captain America was a grand slam home run. "We were up to, after the first issue, close to the million mark, and that was monthly," said Simon. That meant more people were reading *Captain America Comics* than were reading *Time* magazine at the time.[23] Those sales numbers catapulted Captain America up to the same level as DC's Superman and Batman.

> **❝** We were up to, after the first issue, close to the million mark, and that was monthly," said Simon. That meant more people were reading *Captain America Comics* than were reading *Time* magazine at the time.

By the end of the year, Timely comics looked like it was on its way. But one other important event had occurred a couple months before. In November, a skinny teenager was hired by Joe Simon as a temporary office worker—for eight dollars a week.[24] No one—not the teenager, or Goodman, Simon, or Kirby—had any idea of the significance of that decision. But they had just hired the person who would eventually become the main creative force, greatest advocate, and face of Marvel comics for the next seventy-five years.

Temporary Worker?

When Stanley Leiber arrived at Timely Comics in November of 1940, he was a six-foot-tall, skinny, yet somehow handsome, seventeen-year-old kid. He had graduated from high school the previous spring and was looking for a long-term job. His parents, both Romanian immigrants, had struggled financially throughout the Great Depression, and the young Lieber had been encouraged to work hard, skip a grade when possible, and graduate as early as he could so that he could find work to help support his family, a common occurrence those days.

As a kid, Lieber had dreams of becoming a writer, and for a time he worked part-time for a newspaper, writing preliminary obituaries about famous living people, just in case they died.[25] But he soon grew tired of writing about living people as if they were dead. "My uncle, Robbie Solomon, told me they might be able to use someone at the publishing company where he worked," Lieber said. "The idea of being involved in publishing definitely appealed to me." Technically, the kid knew Goodman, the owner, because they were related by marriage.[26] But Goodman was surprised when Lieber was hired. The first time Goodman saw him working in the office, he asked, "What are you doing here?"[27]

Goodman's publishing companies were busy, so Lieber did a little bit of everything. He swept floors, fetched coffee and lunch, erased pencil marks from newly inked artwork, and even did some proofreading.[28] But Lieber quickly earned the trust of his boss, Joe Simon. "Sometimes in proofreading I'd say, 'You know, this sentence doesn't sound right. It ought to be written like this,'" Lieber recalled. "Well, go ahead and change it!" would be the response.

It wasn't long before Lieber got a chance to write something: a text-only filler story called "Captain America Foils the Traitor's Revenge." But the kid decided not to use his real name as the byline. Years later, he claimed that he was saving "Stanley Lieber" for when he published the great American novel. Instead, he used a name he made up: Stan Lee. It was the name he would be known by the rest of his life.

> It wasn't long before Lieber got a chance to write something: a text-only filler story called "Captain America Foils the Traitor's Revenge." But the kid decided not to use his real name as the byline. Years later, he claimed that he was saving "Stanley Lieber" for when he published the great American novel. Instead, he used a name he made up: Stan Lee. It was the name he would be known by the rest of his life.

More Comic Books—And a New Editor

In 1941, Martin Goodman's companies made the shift; they were producing more comic books than pulp magazines.[29] That kept the small staff busy, having to create every story from scratch. With the ever-increasing workload in the comic book department, Lee took on more and more assignments. Simon was still writing, editing, and contributing to the artwork. Kirby, who drew furiously, was named artistic director. The companies also hired freelancers. Another artist, Syd Shores, was hired to help with the inking.[30] And Lee wrote and wrote. Each month Goodman's companies released new comic books, sometimes as many as three different titles at once.

The pace was frantic, and conflicts arose between Goodman and his lead artists, Simon and Kirby. When they left the company in a dispute, Goodman made a move that was probably a surprise to everyone, including Stan Lee. Goodman named the teenager, who possessed only one year of experience, the editor in chief of Timely Comics. "Martin put me in charge 'temporarily' until he could find a replacement," Lee remembered. But Martin never did replace him.

"He was a young kid," said Timely artist Vince Fago about Lee at first. "To him writing was like talking, and he used to love to talk." Fago also said Lee was "absolutely nonconformist, but a very wonderful guy." He described how Lee used to work. He'd write a page, and then call a freelance artist to dictate it to him over the phone. He'd write more and call again, telling him every part of the story until it was done. And he'd always be working on multiple stories at the same time. "He'd work with about three or four people, giving them parts of [different] stories," said Fago, who concluded with a clear understatement: "He was very good."[31]

Even when World War II started and Lee joined the army, he continued writing comic books for Goodman. When the war was over, he returned to New York and resumed his position as Timely Comics' editor in chief.

A Timely Routine

Just twenty-one when he was discharged by the army, Lee was by then a seasoned comic book veteran with a lot of writing experience. He oversaw a creative staff that had grown to twenty artists. They gathered in a large office they called the bullpen, where they worked together, gave one another tips, discussed stories, and argued about New York's baseball teams: the Yankees and the Dodgers. Lee gave the artists assignments, trying to keep them happy, and making sure the whole comic book production process kept moving. And of course, he kept writing. He loved the creative part—coming up with characters, generating plots, and writing dialogue. It fed the machine, but sometimes Lee wondered if that machine was actually taking him somewhere.[32]

That role of businessman was fulfilled by Goodman, and the separation between him and the artists, with Lee overseeing the creative side, is one of the reasons they were successful. "Martin Goodman never came in to speak to the artists," said Allen Bellman, a Timely staff artist in the 1940s.[33] Stan Goldberg, who worked at Marvel in the forties and fifties, concurred. "Martin Goodman left it all up to Stan," noted Goldberg. "Stan would have to get okays from Goodman, but that was about it. . . . I very rarely saw him. I don't think Martin ever came into Stan's office, and I never saw him in the bullpen."[34]

Goodman was content with this arrangement and settled into a routine. He came to the office every day, but he spent a lot of his time there playing Scrabble. Every afternoon he took a nap on his office couch. And he often played golf, not only out of enjoyment for the game, but also to keep his finger on the pulse of what others in publishing were doing.

Today the creators of intellectual property seek to own and control what they create. Back then, most artist and writers didn't think that way. Coming out of the Great Depression, they tended to be more like Lee, focusing on making an income. "I've never been one of these people who worries about [who owns the intellectual property]," Lee said. "I should have been. I'd be wealthy now, if I had been. I always felt the publisher was the guy investing all his money, and I was working for the publisher, and whatever I did belonged to him. That was the way it was. And I was always treated well, I got a good salary. I was not a businessman."[35]

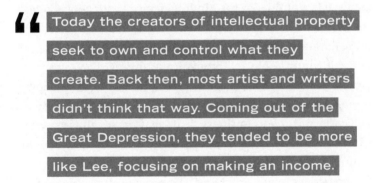

Today the creators of intellectual property seek to own and control what they create. Back then, most artist and writers didn't think that way. Coming out of the Great Depression, they tended to be more like Lee, focusing on making an income.

Goodman and Lee maintained this arrangement from the time the war ended, through the forties and fifties, and on into the sixties. Trends came and went during those years. Superheroes declined in the forties. Captain America, the biggest superhero in Timely's arsenal, ended his run in 1950. Timely published more titles trying to appeal to girls. War comics came into vogue during the Korean War. Science fiction became bigger. So did horror.

A Dark Time for Comics

In the 1950s, comic books came under fire after psychiatrist Fredric Wertham wrote an article in *Saturday Review of Literature* stating that comic books were a negative influence on children and contributed to juvenile delinquency. He followed that in 1954 with a book called *Seduction of the Innocent*. Wertham campaigned against comic books and was critical of those focused on horror, crime, and war. He especially hated superheroes. The Senate even held hearings to investigate comic books. After that, comic book publishers made efforts to regulate themselves, similar to the way the movie industry had since the 1930s with the Hays Code, or the Motion Picture Production Code, a set of rules American filmmakers voluntarily followed for decades, limiting subject matter and its expression. But the popularity of comic books fell dramatically anyway. The sales from Goodman's comic book division dropped from 15 million a month in 1953 to 4.6 million in 1955.[36] To survive, Goodman cut costs and made business deals that drastically restricted what he could publish. At one point, he ordered Lee to fire his entire staff, leaving only Lee on the payroll.

"It was very tough," said Lee. "These were all people that I'd work with. I knew their families. And I was asked to let everybody go. I don't know why Goodman kept me on. I guess he just felt that if there was a chance at all he wouldn't give up the comics completely."[37]

Goodman's company was publishing only a few titles, and they were less than inspired. Lee was discouraged with what he was writing. Beginning to think he was in a dead-end career, he wondered, "Where was I going? I couldn't use words of more than two syllables or create complicated plots—the good guy had to be all good, the bad guy all bad. I hated that."[38] He thought about quitting. If he had, Marvel Studios might have died before it ever began. But then something happened. It was a spark that would ignite a big bang in the Marvel Universe.

> **❝** I was asked to let everybody go. I don't know why Goodman kept me on. I guess he just felt that if there was a chance at all he wouldn't give up the comics completely.❞

Lee received advice that he decided to take. If he hadn't, Goodman's comic book division might have died a slow and inglorious death. And there certainly would never have been a Marvel Studios, because its greatest and most popular characters would never have come to life.

"There was an idea . . . called the Avengers Initiative."

—NICK FURY

CHAPTER ONE

THE BIRTH OF A NEW GENERATION OF SUPER-HEROES

In 1960, Stan Lee was editing five teen humor titles, two romances, four westerns, one war comic, and four monster story titles.[1] And he wasn't happy about it. "The various monster stories that made up the bulk of our production at that time were beginning to pale for me, and probably for the readers, too," said Lee. "The titles were no longer selling the large numbers they once did. As far as I could tell, the comic book industry was in trouble. There was nothing new coming along to pique the readers' interest. I felt we were merely doing the same type of thing, over and over again, with no hope of either greater financial rewards or creative satisfaction."[2]

Lee had finally had enough. One day in the summer of 1961, he decided he was done with comic books and Goodman organization. "I felt I'd been there too long," Lee said, "and I wanted to leave. I figured I could always get a writing job of some kind."[3] He planned to tell his boss that afternoon. But before the disillusioned editor could say a word, Martin Goodman came into Lee's office and exclaimed, "Stan, can you come up with a team of superheroes like the Justice League?"

Goodman had just come back from playing golf with the publisher of National Comics. As always, Goodman was alert for any information that might clue him in on a coming trend. Nation's publisher mentioned in passing that a new series, *The Justice League of America*, had been introduced at DC, featuring Superman, Batman, and Wonder Woman, and it was selling surprisingly well. Goodman suspected that meant interest in superheroes might be on the rise, and he wanted to capitalize on it.

"Martin caught me off guard with his enthusiasm for creating a new superhero title," Lee remembered. "He was so fired up about it that I couldn't bring myself to tell him I wanted out. I decided to let it go till the next day."

Lee went home intending to get out of the comic book business. But when he discussed it with his wife, Joanie, she encouraged him to try something different.

"You know, Stan," Lee recalled her saying, "if Martin wants you to create a new group of superheroes, this could be a chance for you to do it the way you've always wanted to. You could dream up plots that have more depth and substance to them, and create characters who have interesting personalities, who speak like real people. It might be fun for you to create brand-new heroes and write them in a different style, the style you've always wanted to use, one that might attract older readers as well as the young ones." Lee often said that Goodman wanted his comic books pitched to six- or seven-year olds.

"Remember, you've got nothing to lose by doing the book your way," Joan continued. "The worst that can happen is that Martin will get mad and fire you; but you want to quit anyway, so what's the risk? At least you'll have gotten it out of your system."[4]

> **This could be a chance for you to do it the way you've always wanted to. You could dream up plots that have more depth and substance to them, and create characters who have interesting personalities, who speak like real people."**

This was exactly what Lee had been wanting to do. Goodman wanted a team, but Lee was determined not to do an imitation of DC's Justice League. Plus, he wanted to move away from what Timely had always done. Lee said he wanted to make the unreal real, by creating more complex plots and trying to avoid many of the clichés that were common to comic book superheroes. His characters would be more like real people. Sure, they had superpowers, but they had flaws. They had personal and relational problems. They experienced internal conflict, which wasn't typically shown at that time. And they dealt with real-world situations. They might be able to solve their superhero problems by using their superpowers, but they would still have to deal with day-to-day problems the way ordinary people did. Lee believed that would make the characters and stories more relatable to everyone.

Fantastic

Lee spent days scribbling notes, trying out characters, and playing with ideas. Finally, he landed on four characters he thought might fit the bill, and he called them the Fantastic Four. The leader of the group was Reed Richards, who immodestly called himself Mr. Fantastic. Lee said of Richards, "He was bright, he was heroic, but he was also a bore."[5] Ben Grimm, called the Thing, was a humorous semi-monster.[6] The female lead character, Susan Storm, was Lee's attempt to avoid stereotypes and the clichés. "Instead of the girl being the girlfriend of the hero who always had to be rescued and didn't know that the mild-mannered hero was really the super-hero, I gave the Invisible Girl a super-power equal to the others—she was the hero's fiancée and an active partner."[7] Rounding out the group was Johnny Storm, Susan's brother. He was the Human Torch (different from the 1939 version). Lee said he "wasn't that nice a guy, he always felt he was wasting his time—since he wasn't getting paid, he'd really rather be modifying his Chevy or chasing girls."[8]

Lee wrote a two-page summary of the characters and the basic plot and gave it to artist Jack Kirby to draw. "I figured the Fantastic Four would be my swan song. I had no idea it would catch on the way it did." Lee said.[9] "I was just trying to get it out of my system once and for all."[10]

> **I figured the Fantastic Four would be my swan song. I had no idea it would catch on the way it did. . . . I was just trying to get it out of my system once and for all."**

It turned out to be a new beginning for Lee—and for Timely Comics. Even before the sales figures were reported, which usually took months after a title appeared on shelves, Lee was receiving fan mail. That had never happened in his twenty-year career. Readers loved *Fantastic Four #1* (November 1961 issue), and they were telling him they wanted more.

The Fantastic Four opened the creative floodgates for Lee. "The characters just ran through Stan's mind like crazy, one after the other," said Joan. "It was a fantastic period."[11]

The Marvel Method

Most of the characters now familiar to moviegoers in the recent blockbuster Marvel films were created from 1961 to 1967. Often, Lee would come up with the idea for a character and a plot and give the overview to an artist, such as Jack Kirby. Kirby would then take it the next several steps. He would create how the character looked. He would draw the panels, fleshing out the plot and capturing the action. Lee or another staff member, such as his brother Larry Lieber, would write the dialogue and captions for each panel. Then it would be inked and colored. This collaborative process became known as the Marvel method.

People argue today about who really created which characters during this period, but it can be difficult to figure out. As Lee said, "A lot of people put something together, and nobody really knows who created it. They're just working on it, y'know?"

At this time there was a growing team of people working on a lot of content, and they kept producing winners. In 1962, Ant-Man, the Incredible Hulk, Thor, and Spider-Man appeared in comic books for the first time. That didn't happen without some resistance from Goodman. He liked the sales figures when comic books sold, but he still had a very narrow view of what should be in them. Lee told Goodman he wanted to create a superhero who was a teenager with spider powers. "I was told in chapter and verse by the fellow who was then my publisher," said Lee of Goodman, "that it was the worst idea he'd ever heard. People hate spiders! You can't call a hero Spider-Man! Stan, don't you understand that teenagers can only be sidekicks?"[12]

> **" I was told in chapter and verse by the fellow who was then my publisher that it was the worst idea he'd ever heard. People hate spiders! You can't call a hero Spider-Man! Stan, don't you understand that teenagers can only be sidekicks?"**

Cracking the Code

But Lee had already cracked the code. "You ask the audience to suspend disbelief and accept that some idiot can climb on walls, but once that's accepted, you ask: What would life be like in the real world if there were such a character? Would he still have to worry about dandruff, about acne, about getting girlfriends, about keeping a job?"[13]

Lee found a way to move forward with Spider-Man anyway. Since Goodman wanted Lee to discontinue one of their titles that wasn't doing well, *Amazing Adult Fantasy,* Lee stuck his story of Spider-Man into its final issue. "When you're doing the last issue of a magazine you're about to kill, nobody really cares what you put in it. So I figured I'd get Spider-Man out of my system."[14]

Spider-Man was a huge hit with readers, and he would go on to become the face of Marvel. The character would star in movies that would make more $6.36 *billion!*[15]

Lee got a lot more "out of his system" the next year. In 1963 he and his team created Iron Man, Nick Fury, Doctor Strange, and the Wasp. The X-Men also appeared for the first time, with Professor Charles Xavier, Magneto, Cyclops, Beast, Angel, Iceman, Marvel Girl, Mastermind, Quicksilver, Toad, and Scarlet Witch. Lee originally didn't want to call them the X-Men. He wanted to call them "The Mutants," but Goodman overruled him, saying he didn't think the readers of his comic books would know what that word meant.[16] Lee also introduced the Avengers that year, with Iron Man, Hulk, Thor, Ant-Man, and the Wasp. In 1964, he revived Captain America and had him join the group. Black Widow, Hawkeye, and Daredevil also debuted.

Starting in the early sixties, the comic book company that started as Timely (and was at one time known as Atlas) finally became Marvel. Beginning in June of 1961, the small initials *MC* started to appear inside a small rectangle on the cover of their comic books. In May 1963, *Marvel Comics Group* branding began appearing on covers.

Lee also began inserting himself into the comic books in a more personal way. He started writing an editorial piece he called "Stan's Soapbox," where he commented on social issues, such as racism or drug abuse. He asked fans to write in with their reactions to characters and stories. And he started to publish credits for writers, artists, inkers, letterers, colorists, and editors, which was unusual.[17]

After years of being disillusioned, he was excited again. He especially loved breaking new ground and pushing the envelope of the genre. Pop culture critic Richard Harrington pointed out that "Marvel in the early '60s . . . established a reputation for breaking new ground. 'Daredevil' was the first blind super-hero; black super-heroes Black Panther (1968) and Luke Cage (1972) helped break the color line with their own series, while 'Sgt. Fury and His Howling Commandos' (1963) had featured the comic world's first ethnic platoon with a black (Gabriel Jones), a Jew (Izzy Cohen), and an Italian (Dino Manelli)."[18]

Dealmaker

While Lee was hard at work writing and leading the artists at Marvel, Martin Goodman was trying to figure out how to better capitalize on it. In 1968 he sold his entire publishing enterprise, called Magazine Management Company, to a conglomerate called Perfect Film and Chemical Corporation, later renamed Cadence Industries.[19] Goodman received slightly less than $15 million, which was just under the amount of Magazine Management's annual sales, plus he also received some bonds. As part of the deal, Goodman also signed a contract to work as president and publisher of the division. And his son Chip, whom Goodman had groomed to be his successor, signed on to be editorial director. Cadence also wanted Lee to sign a contract to stay on as editor in chief of Marvel,[20] which Lee did.[21]

For the next four years, Marvel Comics chugged along, but then comic book sales began to decline again. Goodman was still running the business side of things, as he always had. Lee kept writing using the Marvel method, as well as overseeing all the artwork and editing all the comic books.

In 1972 at the age of sixty-four, Goodman retired as president and publisher. He had planned for his son Chip to take his place, but when he stepped down, Cadence named Lee the new publisher and president, believing that he was Marvel's secret sauce. Goodman was furious, so much so that in 1974, he started another comic book company to compete with Marvel. He called it Atlas Comics and put Chip in charge of it. Goodman even hired Lee's brother, Larry Lieber, as a member of is staff, since Leiber had done a lot of writing for Lee at Marvel. But Atlas Comics didn't last. It folded after only a year.[22]

Stan Lee's Phase Two

After thirty years as the editor of Marvel's comic books, Lee finally had a chance to take Marvel in a new direction. As he stepped up to become the president and publisher, he ended his long-time tenure as editor in chief. And he was excited. In a September 1972 "Bullpen Bulletin." Lee wrote, "It's time for Phase Two to begin. Marvel's still much too young, too zingy, to bright-eyed and bushy-tailed to settle back and bask in the sun of yesterday's success. . . . If you think we turned you on before, the best is yet to be—wait'll you see what's coming! . . . Marvel's on the move again!"[23]

Lee wanted to take Marvel to the next level, and that included putting Marvel's characters on the screen in Hollywood. He said he wanted to "make it the next Disney."[24]

His first goal was to try to make Marvel a household name. "The one thing I always thought our company lacked was the right type of promotion," said Lee. "We had heroes whom our readers loved; we had enthusiasts who couldn't wait for the next issues of their favorite titles; we had as solid a corps of fans as any company could hope for; but we never had a meaningful program in place for promoting or publicizing our product. Except for our fans, most of the outside world seemed blissfully unaware of us."[25]

> " Marvel's still much too young, too zingy, too bright-eyed and bushy-tailed to settle back and bask in the sun of yesterday's success. . . . If you think we turned you on before, the best is yet to be."

Lee started traveling across the country to speak to audiences every week. While Goodman had always been a quiet businessman in search of a "nice profit," Lee was a natural showman. With his editorials in Stan's Soapbox, he had been like a sideshow barker calling to his readers. Now he would become a ringmaster of Marvel's circus of wonderous superheroes. His main target audience was university students. He averaged a speaking gig a week and even traveled internationally to promote Marvel. "I really think I had some effect," said Lee. "A groundswell just kept growing and growing."[26]

However, when Lee wasn't traveling, speaking, and promoting, he had new obligations that kept him busy. He was often stuck in corporate meetings talking about the financials and business strategy. It wore on him. "I suddenly realized that I'm doing something that millions of people can do better than I do. The thing I enjoy—the creative stuff—I'm not doing anymore."[27] Where he had always been insulated from the financial side of the business, now he was responsible for it. Cadence

Industries expected Marvel to make a good profit for the corporation, but in the 1970s, that was an uphill battle. Comic book sales were sliding again—and getting worse. Not even Lee's energy and optimism could turn Marvel's situation around. After only two years, Lee stepped down as president, but kept his position as publisher.

Marvel would go through a series of editors. The role of president was stabilized a little more quickly, though the first president who replaced Lee didn't last long. Jim Galton became president in 1975 and remained in that role for fifteen years until he retired.[28] But the comic book business looked like it might not survive. Marvel's editors tried a little bit of everything in an attempt to spur sales. They brought in people who had worked in underground comics to try to appeal to the counterculture. They introduced a flood of new characters and rebooted old ones, but sales continued to slide. "Nobody bought comics. It was a dying industry, and we knew it," said a Marvel writer and editor who had started with the comic book company as an intern. "We all figured by 1980 we'd all be out looking for a real job."[29]

Change in Focus

When you're a comic book company that doesn't make money selling comic books, even after experimenting with characters and stories, what do you do? Leverage your intellectual property in other ways. For the first time, Marvel made a concerted effort to generate revenue by licensing its characters to toy manufactures and entertainment companies.

This was mostly new territory for Marvel. Back in 1966, Marvel had licensed the rights to Captain America, Iron Man, Hulk,

Thor, and Sub-Mariner to Grantray-Lawrence Animation so that they could create *The Marvel Super Heroes*, a children's cartoon for television, but that was about it.[30] The deal had only one purpose: to sell more comic books. But now Cadence wanted to get Marvel characters into movies and on television.

When they began looking into the prospect of licensing Marvel's intellectual property to the entertainment industry, they ran into a problem. They learned that years before in 1971, Chip Goodman, a true student of his father's business practices, had already sold the film rights to nearly *all* of Marvel's characters. Steve Lemberg, the young concert promoter who bought them, said. "The only decision that Chip ever made was to give me all the rights to his comic books. They gave me a twenty-page contract with interlocking rights and options; I could do anything I wanted. I could make movies, records, anything." And what did Chip Goodman receive for all this? A paltry $2,500. And Lemberg also had the right to renew the contract indefinitely with full, exclusive creative control of the characters.[31] One Marvel employee said that Chip thought of the $2,500 as found money.[32] By "finding" $2,500, how many millions of dollars in opportunities had he lost? Fortunately, Cadence Industries' lawyers worked out a way to get back the rights from Lemberg. Marvel was back in the game.

With the rights secured again, Lee worked to promote Marvel characters in any way he could in both New York and Hollywood. When rock group The Who's *Tommy* was a hit in 1975, Lee wrote a treatment for a rock opera featuring the Fantastic Four.[33] He took a stab at Broadway when he wrote out ideas for a show with Captain America. He created TV plots with Daredevil and Black Widow, movie treatments for Ghost Rider, Howard the Duck, and the Sub-Mariner. He pushed the idea of a Silver Surfer movie, even approaching Paul McCartney about writing the score. He wrote an outline for a *Godspell*-inspired off-Broadway musical featuring Thor. Writing a description of Thor that seems as though it was anticipating the casting of Chris Hemsworth, Lee described the god of thunder in his outline as having the physique of Arnold Schwarzenegger, the face of Robert Redford, and the voice of voice of Richard Burton.[34]

> **When they began looking into the prospect of licensing Marvel's intellectual property to the entertainment industry, they ran into a problem. In 1971, Chip Goodman had already sold the film rights to nearly *all* of Marvel's characters.**

As Lee pitched ideas, he saw some moderate success. In 1976, Marvel sold live-action film rights for Spider-Man and Hulk to Steve Krantz, and TV rights for Spider-Man to Dan Goldman. Frank Price of Universal Television, intrigued when he saw an image of the Hulk on his son's sweatshirt, sought the character's live-action TV rights. He ended up securing rights to twelve Marvel characters of his choosing for $12,500. Then Price successfully pitched TV shows to CBS featuring eight of those Marvel characters, with the network agreeing to finance a two-hour pilot for each.[35]

The Amazing Spider-Man aired on CBS in 1977, but it was lackluster. "The people doing the Spider-Man show kept writing one bad script after another," Lee said. "So we're either going to have to drop the show or go with bad scripts—I don't know which is worse." Lee complained, "The writers are all a bunch of hacks—the best of them—[are] used to writing TV series with interchangeable plots. The problem is, our characters need specialized plots—they're unique."[36] The Spider-Man TV show ran thirteen episodes and was then canceled.

The next year a Doctor Strange pilot aired on CBS, but it failed to create any television magic and quickly disappeared. A Daredevil pilot was created for ABC but never saw the light of day. The Hulk had better luck in 1978 with the television series *The Incredible Hulk,* starring Bill Bixby and Lou Ferrigno. It ran on CBS for five seasons.[37] That was Marvel's first big success on the small screen.

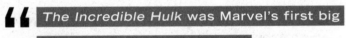

The Incredible Hulk was Marvel's first big success on the small screen.

Big Ideas for the Big Screen

The large screen was a tougher sell than television. Marvel faced two problems in convincing Hollywood to put its characters in movie theaters. The first problem was that Hollywood had a history of not *getting* superheroes or comic books. As Lee talked to producers, it seemed like he was talking to Martin Goodman all over again. Lee kept trying to explain that Marvel's comic book stories were written to and bought by teenagers, college students, and older people. But like Goodman, producers in Hollywood thought anything based on Marvel's comic books should be created for six-year-olds.

A prime example was the way DC's Batman was handled in the TV show that aired in 1966. The series was originally proposed as a cool drama in the vein of the popular *The Man from U.N.C.L.E.* series. But when producer William Dozier was asked to lead the project, he wasn't familiar with Batman and had to go out and buy some comic books to acquaint himself with the superhero. After reading a few stories, Dozier couldn't imagine doing the TV show seriously. Instead he made it a campy, over-the-top self-parody, primarily for kids—with an ironic wink to any adults who might be watching.

The second problem was that the actions of superheroes and villains portrayed on the pages of comic books couldn't be easily duplicated on film at that time. It was challenging to convincingly portray a person swinging between buildings like Spider-Man, transforming like Hulk, bursting into flame like the Human Torch, turning invisible like Susan Storm, or flying like Iron Man.

Some of that changed when Richard Donner's *Superman* starring Christopher Reeve opened in 1978. While the movie had moments of broad comedy, it was not targeted to six-year-olds. And for its time, the special effects were good. *Superman* movie posters proclaimed, "You'll believe a man can fly." And even greater advances in visual effects were being made by Industrial Light and Magic in the late seventies and early eighties.

Even after Stan Lee moved permanently to the Los Angeles area in 1980 to promote his beloved comic book characters, Marvel's executives seemed resigned to take their cue from Hollywood and focus their attention on the children's market. In 1981, Cadence Industries bought DePatie-Freleng Enterprises (DFE Films), an animation studio that created the Pink Panther cartoon and had done a few Marvel projects. Cadence called this new division Marvel Productions and named David H. DePatie president, with Lee serving as its creative director.

Marvel Productions focused on producing children's Saturday morning cartoons.[38]

But Lee wasn't ready to let go of the idea of bringing live-action superheroes to movie screens for adults. He kept pitching ideas, but getting anything done in Hollywood was always a challenge for him. "Nothing is ever definate [sic] out here, and it takes forever to come to any agreement on anything between any two parties," wrote Lee to a movie-director friend.[39]

Lee was accustomed to getting an idea in the morning, writing a plot outline in the afternoon, calling a staff artist that night to describe the character and story to him, and seeing illustrated comic book pages within days or weeks. Then after taking a pass at the dialogue himself, he would pass along the pages to the letterer, and then the printer. The completed comic book would appear on the stands and be in readers hands within a couple of months.

"Out here, you get an idea for a movie and years later, you're still trying to get it on the screen," Lee explained. "Here, it is much more big business. There are contracts and negotiations and turnarounds. I find that a little frustrating, because I like to move fast and write fast."[40]

" Out here, you get an idea for a movie and years later, you're still trying to get it on the screen. Here, it is much more big business. There are contracts and negotiations and turnarounds. I find that a little frustrating, because I like to move fast and write fast."

Hollywood was a place where everyone said yes, but what they really meant was maybe, and what they did was wait to make decisions until they believed they had surefire talent attached: an actor, a director, or a screenwriter with a big box-office appeal and a track record to prove it. And even then, people only moved forward on a project if they could do it with someone else's money. To begin this long and convoluted process, producers bought options on intellectual property which locked it up for a period of time, giving them the exclusive right to use it—just in case they wanted to. Someday. Properties could be in development for years and sometimes even decades.

During this period, Tom Selleck was courted to star in a Doctor Strange movie. Carl Weathers considered playing the superhero Power Man in a film. Irwin Allen wanted to make a movie about the Human Torch. Roger Corman took out an option to make a Spider-Man movie. And animation company Nelvana obtained the rights to create a live-action film with the X-Men.[41] None of these deals or proposals ever amounted to anything.

Wins and Losses

While Marvel's representatives struggled to get traction in Hollywood in the early 1980s, their comic books suddenly began selling again, but not because of anything Cadence was doing. Americans had begun seriously collecting baseball cards in the mid-1970s, thanks to nostalgic baby boomers. At that time, collectors were spending extraordinary sums for rare vintage baseball cards. When people everywhere saw the potential value of collecting, they started looking for items to invest in—not just older items, but products that had actually been manufactured to be "collectable." That included comic books. Soon, comic book shops started to pop up everywhere. People bought vintage comic books from them, but they also started buying new ones too. They looked for particular artists and writers they enjoyed. And Marvel's editorial staff began catering to that market by creating special comic books that they speculated collectors would want. The market had turned.

Meanwhile Jim Galton, the president of Marvel, aggressively pursued licensing deals with toy makers. After Mattel was outbid by Kenner for the rights to DC's characters, including the popular Superman, Batman, and Wonder Woman, Mattel eagerly worked out a deal with Marvel. One of the stipulations of the deal required Marvel to launch a comic book to support the line of toys, and the book's title had to use *Secret Wars* because Mattel's market research showed kids responded well to those two words.[42] When *Marvel Super Heroes Secret Wars* was published in May 1984, it contained virtually all of Marvel's A-list characters: Captain America, Spider-Man, Iron Man, Hulk, Thor, Captain Marvel, Hawkeye, the Wasp, Wolverine, Professor X, Colossus, Thing, and others.[43] For the first time, merchandise drove editorial content for Marvel.

The licensing deals were paying off. By the end of 1985, Marvel's revenues had reached $100 million, driven in large part by licensing agreements for products featuring its characters.[44] But Cadence was experiencing other financial problems that many of Marvel's employees knew nothing about. So they were surprised when one day a man showed up at Marvel's offices in New York and started making comments about the state of the work space. Marvel writer Tom DeFalco, who later became editor in chief, said, "I'm proofreading a comic, and this guy comes in, criticizing the desk and the office décor and everything, and I'm thinking he's an interior designer. I look at him and I say, 'Listen, I don't know who you are, but I've really got to get this book out to the printer.' And he stands up with this big 'Hi, I'm Bob Rehme! I'm president of New World!'"[45] As in New World Pictures.

> " The licensing deals were paying off. By the end of 1985, Marvel's revenues had reached $100 million, driven in large part by licensing agreements for products featuring its characters.

What was the president of a film company doing in Marvel's New York offices? He was looking over his new acquisition. Though Marvel's employees didn't know it at the time, New World owned Marvel. Cadence Industries had gone bankrupt, New World had bought it, and Bob Rehme was DeFalco's—and every other Marvel employee's—new boss.

"Can we put the bickering on hold until after we survive this massive space battle?"

—GAMORA

CHAPTER TWO

THE EPIC BATTLE FOR MARVEL

The trouble for Cadence Industries had begun three years earlier. The eighties was a decade of corporate raiders, hostile takeovers, and company mergers. Starting in 1983, millionaire investor (and now billionaire) Mario Gabelli began buying shares of Cadence Industries to try to gain control of the company. In self-defense, Cadence executives took on short-term debt to buy their company's outstanding shares to protect themselves and prevent a takeover.[1] But Cadence got into trouble financially and eventually had to file for bankruptcy. In November of 1986, New World Entertainment acquired Marvel Comics Group and Marvel Productions for $46 million as part of the liquidation of Cadence Industries.[2] New World renamed them the Marvel Entertainment Group.

Good News . . . and Bad News

The good news was that Marvel was finally connected directly to Hollywood. New World Pictures had been around since 1970. Starting out as a distributor of low budget films, New World had branched out to distribute international films by Ingmar Bergman, Federico Fellini, and Akira Kurosawa. And it also produced low budget films as well as television shows. Some of their movies were very low quality, but some excellent directors got their start with New World, including Academy Award-winner Ron Howard.

But there was bad news too. Marvel's new owners, like its former owners at Cadence Industries, knew nothing about comic books. When the purchase of Marvel was finalized, New World president Bob Rehme told his vice president of marketing, "We just bought Superman."

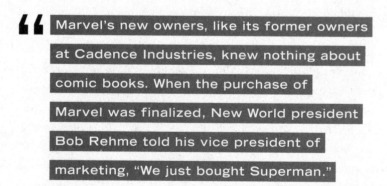

> Marvel's new owners, like its former owners at Cadence Industries, knew nothing about comic books. When the purchase of Marvel was finalized, New World president Bob Rehme told his vice president of marketing, "We just bought Superman."

The vice president evidently *did* know something about comic books and asked if Warner Brothers was selling DC. He knew Superman was a DC superhero.

"No, no, no—we bought Marvel!" Rehme replied.

"No, Bob," the other man responded. "We bought Spider-Man."

Rehme responded with panic. Rehme raced out of his office. "Holy shit," he said. "We gotta stop this. Cannon has the Spider-Man movie!"[3] New World later contacted Cannon to try to get the rights but failed.

The executives never were sure what do with the characters whose rights they retained. This must have been familiar territory to Lee, who was still trying to get Marvel characters on the big screen. Going all the way back to the early days of Marvel superheroes, movie studios hadn't known how to use the comic book characters. In the 1940s, Republic Pictures had made Captain American unrecognizable when they put him into their serials. Captain America was a soldier named Steve Rogers who possessed special superhuman powers thanks to an experiment conducted by the army. He fought with the help of a teenage sidekick named Bucky. His signature weapon was a shield. Who did Republic Pictures present as Captain America? A district attorney named Grant Gardner. He had no affiliation with the army. He possessed no superpowers. He kept his identity secret, and he was assisted by a secretary named Gail. And his weapon? A gun.[4] The movie character was nothing like the comic book character.

New World owned Marvel, but it didn't do anything new or innovative with it. One of New World's script evaluators, who was a comic book fan, observed of New World's executives, "They tended to look down on the titles, gravitating toward projects that made fun of the medium." He tried to explain to his boss, "You've just bought Alaska. You need to dig below the surface and find out what's there." But they didn't. Like their counterparts before them, New World's executives targeted the children's market. With Stan Lee as executive producer, they oversaw the production of half-hour cartoon episodes of *X-Men: The Animated Series,* hoping to sell them to network TV or put them into syndication.[5]

❝❝ You've just bought Alaska. You need to dig below the surface and find out what's there."

The One Marvel Character Who Made it to the Big Screen

The one movie featuring a Marvel character that came out during this period was *Howard the Duck* in 1986, but that had little to do with New World. Beginning in the 1970s, George Lucas was interested in seeing a movie made featuring the character. After he finished filming *Return of the Jedi,* Lucas stepped down as president of Lucasfilm and focused on producing. He acquired the rights to Howard the Duck and hired writers Willard Huyck and Gloria Katz who had worked on *American Graffiti* with him to create a screenplay for an animated movie. But Universal Studios, who agreed to distribute the film, insisted on a live-action version to fill an empty slot in their summer schedule. Lucas agreed and moved forward, making the film with Huyck as the director.[6]

The movie bombed. Movie critics hated it. So did Marvel fans. And it didn't make money. The film's budget was $37 million, but it made only $16.3 million in the U.S. and Canada. The worldwide gross was $37.9.[7] And Universal had spent an additional $8 million on promotion.[8]

The failure of *Howard the Duck* didn't make Marvel properties any more attractive to moviemakers; it ended Huyck's career as a director and it put Lucas into a financial bind. He thought the movie would be a hit and generate a lot of revenue, which he needed because he had just built the $50-million Skywalker Ranch complex. When the movie failed, he needed to raise cash, so he sold some of his assets. One of those was his newly launched computer graphics business, which he sold to Steve Jobs. At least that part of the story had a happy ending. The small company he sold eventually became Pixar Animation Studios.[9]

New World never leveraged Marvel's assets. One former Marvel employee said, "New World didn't want to be in the comic book business, but you couldn't throw the baby out with the bathwater."[10] What they really wanted to do was use the intellectual property to sell products. Among other things, they planned to create Marvel retail stores, following the example of Disney. But when they got short on cash, they scrapped the plan. Then their financial situation got even worse. In January of 1989, New World sold the publishing and licensing arms of Marvel for $82.5 million to MacAndrews and Forbes Holdings, a corporation controlled by Ronald Perelman.[11] But New World held onto Marvel Productions and folded it into New World's TV and Movie business. But in the end, they lost Marvel Productions too. Just three months later, Perelman bought all of New World for $145 million.[12]

From Superheroes to Pawns

The next phase of Marvel's life saw the company bouncing around like a shiny ball in a pinball machine. Perelman, who owned MacAndrews and Forbes, was a wheeler-dealer who bought and sold companies. His most notable business move up until that time had been the acquisition of Revlon in 1985 via a hostile takeover. Perelman's mode of operation was to buy and sell companies, often using other people's money, and making sure he reaped the benefits personally. For his purchase of Marvel, Perelman put in only $10.5 million of his own money. The rest of the $82.5 million was borrowed.[13]

From 1989 when Perelman took over, until 1996, Marvel went through a head-spinning series of changes and machinations designed to benefit the individuals who controlled Marvel, not the company's stockholders, not its employees, and not its comic book-reading fans.

In October of 1990, when longtime Marvel president Jim Galton retired from Marvel, Perelman replaced him with Terry Stewart, an expert in mergers and acquisitions, who also happened to be a comic book fan. Stewart said his focus would be on getting movies made, and he appointed Joe Calamari, a former Cadence executive as chief executive of Marvel Productions. But not much happened in Hollywood.

Under Stewart's leadership Marvel started raising prices on comic books. When sales didn't go down, they planned additional price increases. And they pushed sales hard. Where the sale of 400,000 copies of a new title was considered a home run in the early 1980s, when *X-Force #1* debuted in 1991, it sold nearly 4 million copies.[14]

Marvel's staff was pushed to create more characters, produce more new titles, and generate a greater volume of sales. The editorial staff suffered. Sven Larsen, who was director of marketing at the time, said, "It's hard for people who haven't come up through the comic book industry to understand just how hard it is to get a comic book out."[15] But the truth was that the leadership really didn't seem to care. They were positioning Marvel for an IPO.

> **Marvel's staff was pushed to create more characters, produce more new titles, and generate a greater volume of sales. The editorial staff suffered.**

In the summer of 1991, Marvel went public offering stock that represented 40 percent of the company's value. The stock went from $16.50 to $18 on the first day, trading at a volume of 2.3 million shares.[16] In the months following, the price per share went up more than $40. However, most of the money raised by the IPO went directly to Perelman personally through MacAndrews & Forbes—not to Marvel.[17] He wasn't building the company. He was milking it dry.

Perelman and his team of executives continued to wheel and deal using Marvel as their tool. In 1992, Marvel acquired Fleer, a trading card company, for $265 million, even though the baseball card industry was declining. In fact, collecting of all kinds was losing its luster. Thousands of comic book stores were going out of business. But Perelman and his team kept buying more companies. In 1994, they acquired the Panini Group, a sticker-maker, and in 1995 Skybox, another trading card company.

How was Perelman and his team able to pull this off? By setting up a series of shell corporations and selling junk bonds. The process was so convoluted it would take a forensic account-ant to keep track of it. Perelman's companies were like a series of Russian matryoshka dolls. Perelman owned a holding company called Mafco. Mafco owned MacAndrews and Forbes. MacAndrews and Forbes owned Andrews. Andrews owned Marvel. Perelman also created the companies Marvel III Holdings and Marvel Parent Holdings, which were owned by Andrews. Marvel Parent Holdings owned a newly created company called Marvel Holdings. Confused yet?

> **How was Perelman and his team able to pull this off? By setting up a series of shell corporations and selling junk bonds. Perelman's companies were like a series of Russian matryoshka dolls.**

The Marvel stock that Perelman owned was held and controlled in varying amounts by several of these holding companies. These companies put Marvel stock up as collateral in order to sell junk bonds.[18] At the time, Marvel's executives said their ambition was to make Marvel one of the world's top five licensors.[19] Maybe that was true, but they weren't putting money into Marvel to accomplish this. They were pulling cash out. But as Marvel's sales slid, so did its value. And so did its position in the marketplace. While Perelman was doing all this wheeling and dealing, DC Comics passed Marvel and became the best-selling publisher of comics again.[20]

Buying into the Toy Biz

In 1993, during Perelman's flurry of deals, one of his executives wanted to break ties with a small company it had granted a license to called Toy Biz because the toy company was deemed too small for the big merchandizing plans Marvel possessed. What happened as a result would change the course of Marvel's history and ultimately make its comic book characters successful in the movies.

Toy Biz was owned by Ike Perlmutter. Born in Israel in 1942, Perlmutter had served in the Israeli army and immigrated to the United States at the age of twenty-four with the goal of making his fortune. Perlmutter hustled to become successful. Newly arrived to New York, he offered to recite prayers in Hebrew at funerals in Brooklyn for a fee.[21] He sold toys and cosmetics on the street. He also learned to buy unwanted surplus stock at a deep discount and resell it at a profit.[22] Later he started buying unwanted companies that were going out of business and sold off their assets at a profit. That was his plan when he bought Toy Biz, but then he got the idea that he could make the company profitable. He employed a minimal staff, leased a modest headquarters in New York City instead of owning property, acquired licensing rights, outsourced manufacturing to China, leased warehouse space in Arizona, and concentrated on sales to mass merchandisers. All this enabled Toy Biz to maintain an extremely low overhead. One expert estimated that Toy Biz generated nearly $2 million in annual revenues for each employee in the mid-1990s.[23]

One of those key employees was Avi Arad, said to be "the most successful toy developer in the business."[24] Arad was also an Israeli who had served in the military and later emigrated to the United States. Over the course of a twenty-year career in the toy business, Arad had helped create more than 160 toys for manufacturers such a Mattel, Hasbro, Tyco, Nintendo, and Sega. A creative talent, Arad's specialty was action figures, but he had also designed other popular toys, such as Baby Bubbles and Baby Rollerblade.[25] Arad appreciated Perlmutter's business acumen. Arad said, "He knew all there was to know about extending one modest idea—especially when supported by TV shows, movies, and a large ad campaign—into 'a line' that kept selling for years and years. He was paid royalties totaling about $3 million a year, and sometimes double that amount."[26] In return, Perlmutter liked Arad's informality, independent thinking, and track record of best-selling toys for the biggest companies.[27] Arad rose to the position of CEO of Toy Biz.

When Perlmutter learned that Marvel wanted to break ties with his company, he and Arad made a bold proposal. They offered 46 percent of Toy Biz to Marvel in exchange for an exclusive, perpetual, royalty-free license to create toys using Marvel's characters—plus $7 million in cash and a few stipulations about decision-making and staffing.[28] Toy Biz would benefit because it would no longer have to pay royalties to Marvel, thereby increasing its margins, and Marvel would receive higher returns from toy sales than they otherwise would from a traditional licensing deal.[29] They agreed to make the deal, and in the process, Arad also received a 10 percent stake in the company in addition to his salary.[30]

The Birth of Marvel Films

Perelman turned around and used the Toy Biz stock he had gained to raise money and create Marvel Films as a private entity.

His main goal wasn't to get into the movies industry. That was too risky. He wanted to make money on merchandise that would be created as others made films.[31] He put Arad in place as the new company's president and CEO, and immediately dispatched him to Hollywood to promote Marvel characters and start working deals.

Arad was the perfect person to join Stan Lee in Hollywood. Arad felt genuine passion for Marvel's comics.[32] He said he had read Spider-Man and Iron Man comics in Hebrew as a kid.[33] He thought comic books were an original American art form, like jazz.[34] He understood the characters. He had designed the X-Men toy line for Toy Biz, which had made $30 million in sales.[35] Plus, it was Arad's dream to transition from toymaker to moviemaker.[36] It was the perfect opportunity for him.

> Arad felt genuine passion for Marvel's comics. He said he had read Spider-Man and Iron Man comics in Hebrew as a kid. He thought comic books were an original American art form, like jazz.

The first thing Arad did was join Lee in working on *X-Men: The Animated Series* where he became a vocal executive producer.[37] It soon became the number-one-rated kids' cartoon. With Arad's help, there were eventually deals for X-Men apparel, trading cards, video games, action figures, and Pizza Hut meal deals.[38] By the summer of 1993, Arad had also brokered a deal with 20th Century Fox to make a live-action X-Men movie.[39]

When Arad took over Marvel Films, he also discovered that a low-budget film featuring the Fantastic Four was nearing completion. Evidently producer Bernd Eichinger had obtained an option on the Marvel foursome in 1986. As was typical in a film option contract, the rights were set to expire if principle photography didn't start by a certain date. Eichinger had been struggling to obtain financing for a big-budget film, and had asked for an extension, which was refused. So he came up with the idea of doing a film for only $1 million, just to retain his rights. He contacted low-budget producer Roger Corman for help, and they started filming only three days before the option was scheduled to expire.

Arad foresaw the potential disaster to the brand if a low-budget version of a Marvel mainstay came out just as he was trying to build up Marvel in Hollywood, so he contacted Eichinger and offered to buy back the movie. He later stated that he purchased it "for a couple of million dollars in cash and burned it."[40]

As Avi Arad worked to make deals in Hollywood, Ron Perelman was doing the same back in New York. He raised more money and transformed Marvel Films into Marvel Studios to try to gain more control over filmmaking in Hollywood and get the properties Marvel had licensed out of "development hell"— the place where producers and studios talk endlessly about story lines, scripts, directors, actors, and deals, but never actually start the process of making a movie. The Fantastic Four, X-Men, Daredevil, the Incredible Hulk, Silver Surfer, and Iron Man had all been optioned, and none of them had appeared in a movie. Spider-Man had been in development limbo since the early 1980s. Producers Roger Corman and James Cameron had worked on trying to create a Spider-Man film, and three different studios held rights: Orion, Cannon Films, and Carolco

Pictures. Cannon is reputed to have spent $10 million on development with no success.[41] Eventually, the rights ended up at MGM—or at least, that's what that studio claimed. Spider-Man became a prisoner of litigation for eight years as various studios claimed to hold the rights.[42]

The new Marvel Studios was intended to control preproduction. It wanted to commission scripts, hire directors, and negotiate with stars, putting that entire package together and then turning it over to a big studio partner to shoot the film and distribute it. "When you get into business with a big studio," said Arad, "they are developing a hundred or 500 projects; you get totally lost. That isn't working for us. We're just not going to do it anymore. Period."[43] Arad told a *Variety* reporter, "We are finally on the verge of breaking out. This is our bar mitzvah year in a sense."[44]

> **"** When you get into business with a big studio, they are developing a hundred or 500 projects; you get totally lost. That isn't working for us. We're just not going to do it anymore. Period."

At the request of Perelman, Arad was also working a deal with Universal Studios in Orlando to create a Marvel area in Islands of Adventure. Arad hoped to work with their movie division in the future. Perelman hoped to make a deal for quick cash. He accepted $500,000 for letting Universal Studio's use Marvel's name and another $500,000 a year for ten years starting in 1999.[45]

The Slide

But Marvel wasn't doing well. In 1995, Marvel ended the year in the red. Perelman laid off 275 of Marvel's 1,700 employees in January of 1996.[46] But things only got worse and soon came to a head. Over the course of his tenure running Marvel, Perelman had racked up a lot of debt, and creditors were beginning to circle, looking for a chance to take over the company. One of those creditors was Carl Icahn, another corporate raider, who had bought up a third of the bonds Marvel had issued.[47]

Perelman made a move to buy the remainder of Toy Biz and merge it with Marvel, hoping to put Marvel into a better financial position. But Marvel continued to suffer losses. Its debt was downgraded, its stock value fell, and after Perelman tried to enrich himself one more time in the Toy Biz merger, stockholders filed suit against him.[48]

To protect his position against Icahn, and to try to undermine Perlmutter's position as exclusive rights license holder for Marvel toys, Perelman had Marvel file for bankruptcy in December of 1996.[49] Ronald Perelman, Carl Icahn, and the banks who owned much of Marvel's debt fought over control of the company in bankruptcy court for a year. Perlmutter also bought some of Marvel's debt, which gave him a place at the table with the other creditors, since it was possible that he could lose everything.

According to the judge in the bankruptcy case, Perelman had issued junk bonds totaling nearly a billion dollars of debt for Marvel. Between the dividend he had received when the company went public and the payouts to his personally owned holding companies when he issued the bonds, Perelman had pulled $302 million out of Marvel for his personal gain.[50]

The fight for Marvel was bitter and protracted. Perelman made proposals, which were fought by Icahn and the other debt holders. At one point the court gave Icahn control, and it looked like he would win the battle. When Icahn found out Perlmutter and Arad had bought debt to protect themselves, he had Arad fired from his position as head of Marvel Films.[51] But Perlmutter and Arad kept fighting. Arad made a speech to the banks who were part of the bankruptcy case. He said,

> We live in one of the most creative countries in the world. But look around you and see how few characters have been introduced and survived. You have *Star Wars*, maybe *Star Trek*, and you'll be hard-pressed to name any other characters that survived that long. I feel certain that Spider-Man alone is worth a billion dollars. But now, at this crazy juncture, you're going to take 380 million—whatever it is from Carl Icahn—for the whole thing? *One* thing is worth a billion! We have the X-Men. We have the Fantastic Four. They can all be movies.[52]

" Spider-Man alone is worth a billion dollars. . . . We have the X-Men. We have the Fantastic Four. They can all be movies."

In the end, it was a deal put together by Ike Perlmutter that won the day. Toy Biz paid $3.5 million of Icahn's legal costs and granted him general release from litigation. Icahn promised not to take legal action against Toy Biz."[53] Toy Biz agreed to purchase Marvel from the banks, using a bridge loan they would acquire. And in June of 1998, Marvel Enterprises merged with Toy Biz to become the Marvel Entertainment Group with Perlmutter as CEO.

Perlmutter and Arad had saved Marvel from the brink. They were free to take the company forward. And the road was finally clear again for Arad to go back to work getting Marvel superheroes on movie screens.

"Just don't do anything I would do, and definitely don't do anything I wouldn't do. There's a little gray area in there, and that's where you operate."

—TONY STARK TO PETER PARKER

CHAPTER THREE

MARVEL SUPER- HEROES FLY INTO HOLLYWOOD

As soon as Ike Perlmutter gained control of Marvel Enterprises, he began looking for ways to save money and pay off the $200 million in debt he had incurred to satisfy the bankruptcy settlement. He was infamously frugal. One of the first things he did was sell Fleer and Skybox at a loss to be rid of them and scrape together some cash.[1] He reduced the number of editors working for Marvel Comics. He instituted policies at Marvel to limit expenses and worked to terminate contracts with expensive executives.[2] He also pushed Arad to pursue licensing deals.[3] The joke around Marvel was, "If Ike Perlmutter had his way, Marvel would consist of one guy in an office with a phone, licensing the characters."[4]

The licensing efforts were helped in 1998 when the first Marvel superhero feature film opened: *Blade*, starring Wesley

Snipes as a vampire hunter. The rights for this character had been licensed to New Line Cinema, and production had begun in 1997 with a budget of $45 million. Blade was a minor character who first appeared in Marvel's *Tomb of Dracula #10* published in 1973.[5] The film was a surprise hit, earning $17 million on its opening weekend, $70 million in the U.S. and Canada, and a total of $131 million worldwide.[6]

> **The joke around Marvel was, "If Ike Perlmutter had his way, Marvel would consist of one guy in an office with a phone, licensing the characters."**

Marvel Enterprises received only $25,000 in profits from *Blade*, a pittance compared to the debt they needed to retire. But it was a breakthrough. Arad finally had evidence he could use to convince Hollywood to take Marvel characters seriously. "Blade was the least likely to succeed," noted Arad. There were factors that limited some audiences. It was from a comic book. The main character was relatively unknown. The genre was horror. The star was African American. And it was rated R. But it was still a hit. "That was the first time it seemed clear to Hollywood that the Marvel franchise was something special."[7] With Marvel Entertainment under his and Perlmutter's control and the first box-office success of a Marvel superhero, Arad was ready to take the company to the next level.

When he first hit Hollywood, getting anyone to listen had been a struggle. "I was basically climbing a rock straight up back then," Arad said. "It was me almost getting to the top and roll right back down because the industry did not consider comic books to be source material. You know, it was a rough ride and you had to believe in it to try and convince people. Studios actually were the hardest to convince. . . . It was hard to get studios to ever look at a comic book and even when they did they couldn't see it."[8] And while the bankruptcy was being settled, licensing deals had dried up.

Now the situation was looking more promising. But the company still needed cash. As the rights to Spider-Man were becoming untangled, Marvel approached Sony and offered them the film rights to nearly all of Marvel's characters for $25 million.[9] Sony rejected the offer; they said they were only interested in Spider-Man. Arad and Perlmutter looked for other potential takers in Hollywood, but found none. They went back to Sony to work out a deal, asking for $20 million for Spider-Man. They finally came to an agreement: Marvel would receive $10 million to license Spider-Man to Sony, plus Marvel would receive 5 percent of revenue from the movie, which would be produced by Sony's Columbia Pictures division. But Marvel would have to give up some of its revenue from toys, splitting Spider-Man merchandizing revenue with Sony 50-50.[10]

" Blade . . . was the first time it seemed clear to Hollywood that the Marvel franchise was something special."

Next Step with X-Men

In 1999, Twentieth Century Fox began filming *X-Men*. The budget was set at $75 million. That was $30 million more than the budget for *Blade*, but it was still significantly less than most of the big-budget action movies being made at that time. Pre-production was a struggle. The screenplay had gone through 28 drafts with a number of writers, including Joss Whedon, who would later direct a Marvel movie.[11] And Hugh Jackman, who played the major character Wolverine, wasn't cast until three weeks *after* shooting had already started.[12]

Bryan Singer was directing. Originally, he declined the invitation to direct—multiple times. He thought comic books were "unintelligent literature." But he was talked into taking the gig when he read some of the X-Men comic books and watched the animated series that Arad had participated in producing. In the end, Singer connected with the themes of prejudice and discrimination he found in X-Men,[13] and he wanted to tap into the idea of mutants as outsiders.[14] But he also wanted to leave behind some of the things that were in the original comic books, such as the colorful matching superhero uniforms.

Avi Arad and Stan Lee often consulted with Singer, giving him advice on the characters and the comic book world of X-Men. They wanted to help him stay true to the spirit of the source material as he worked to put it on screen. Also on set was producer Lauren Shuler Donner, who had helped to put together the deal with Fox. She had an assistant in his mid-twenties who knew the X-Men comic books well and wanted to see certain aspects of the comic books come to life in the movie. That assistant's name was Kevin Feige. And he would become an important figure in Marvel's history.

Influential Assistant

Born in Boston, Feige grew up in Westfield, New Jersey. The only thing he ever wanted to do was work in movies, so he applied to USC because it was the alma mater of his favorite directors, such as George Lucas, Ron Howard, and Robert Zemeckis. While he did get into USC, his application to their School of Cinematic Arts was rejected—five times. Friends and family tried to convince him to choose another major, but he wouldn't think of it. He applied one more time, and finally got in.[15]

As he was starting film school, he realized that the sharpest students were getting internships. While they didn't pay any money, they did provide college credit and the kind of invaluable experience needed to get in the door in Hollywood. Feige went looking to see what internships were posted, and he spotted one that said Donner/Shuler-Donner Productions. Feige knew about Richard Donner because of *Goonies*, *Lethal Weapon*, and *Superman*, which Feige has called "the most perfect superhero movie." He immediately applied, and a few days later got a position as an intern for Shuler Donner.[16]

During his final semester he was asked to stay on as a paid production assistant—the lowest rung on the Hollywood totem pole. And when he graduated, they gave him his pick of two great opportunities: both Richard Donner and Lauren Shuler Donner needed assistants. He would choose who he wanted to work for.[17]

Feige later recounted, "If I had been asked that question on my first day two years earlier I would've said, "Richard Donner! He's a director! I want to be a director! It's Richard Donner."[18] But he realized that the life of a director had a lot of gaps when he wasn't working. "Lauren on the other hand was in the office every day, developing multiple projects and producing multiple movies," said Feige. He chose Shuler Donner. "Noticing that the people who were higher up in the company used to be her assistants, I considered myself very lucky that Lauren brought me on in that role.[19]

For Shuler Donner, Feige worked on *Volcano* and *You've Got Mail* where he taught Meg Ryan how to use email.[20] As Shuler Donner worked on *X-Men*, Feige, who was already a huge comic book fan, took it upon himself to read all of the X-Men comics. As the screenplay for *X-Men* was being developed, Feige would write notes in response. "Because Lauren is an amazing mentor and is so gracious," said Feige, "she would read the notes. Eventually, she started saying, 'Hey, come into the office and sit with me.' I would be sitting with Tom DeSanto, who's the producer of *X-Men*, and Bryan Singer, who was the newly hired director, and I just started to become a part of that creative team."[21]

Styling Wolverine

On one of the early days on set, Feige got involved as a stylist worked on Hugh Jackman's hair. Knowing the comic books so well, Feige wanted the hair to be more like the odd swept-up style Wolverine had in the comic, and Feige pushed the stylist to keep making it more exaggerated.

"Fine!" Feige recalled the stylist saying in exasperation, "and did a ridiculous version. If you go back and look at it, he's got big-ass hair in that first movie. But that's Wolverine!"[22] Feige went on to become an associate producer on the film and made an impression on Arad, who hired him to work with studios and filmmakers in the future to consult on how best to depict Marvel's characters.[23]

Originally slated for a Christmas 2000 release, *X-Men* was bumped up to June 2000 when Twentieth Century Fox had an unexpected hole in their schedule and didn't have a big-budget summer movie ready to go there as planned.[24] When *X-Men* got put into that slot, it made more than $54 million on opening weekend, and went on to gross $157 million in the U.S. and Canada, and more than $296 million worldwide.[25]

Arad persuaded Perlmutter to attend the premier, which was held on Ellis Island. To Arad, it was like a dream come true. "Two immigrants, Ike and me, who have finally made it, go to Ellis Island. Our boat's passing the Statue of Liberty. It's the American dream!"[26] But to Perlmutter, it was a disaster. Because the timing had been pushed up, the toys they had planned to put on sale in conjunction with the movie weren't ready. In addition, the pre-bankruptcy deal Arad had made didn't give Marvel any part of the box office.[27] And the storyline in the film didn't correspond to the current comic books, so it didn't increase comic book sales either.[28] Marvel missed whatever cross-promotional opportunities that might have been available.

> **"** Arad persuaded Perlmutter to attend the premier, which was held on Ellis Island. To Arad, it was like a dream come true. "Two immigrants, Ike and me, who have finally made it, go to Ellis Island. Our boat's passing the Statue of Liberty. It's the American dream!"

As Arad continued to do deals in Hollywood, back in New York, the editorial and writing staff fought over the comic books.[29] Stan Lee and Steve Ditko argued about who *really* created Spider-Man.[30] And Perlmutter searched for ways to make Marvel profitable.

Comic Book Readers Who Are Movie Makers

Fortunately, a shift began to occur around this same time. Some people in Hollywood actually *wanted* to make films based on comic books. Arad said, "The good news was that it was a time where the kids who just went to art school, or went to writing school, or went to filmmaking school, and so on, they were the ones who actually loved the comic book culture, and many of them were just beginning."[31] Filmmakers who loved comic books were chatting up Marvel editors at parties, looking for ways to get access to content.[32]

One of those comic book lovers was Sam Raimi, who was slated to direct *Spider-Man*. An avid comic book reader, he owned a collection of more than 25,000 comic books and was a fan specifically of Spider-Man.[33]

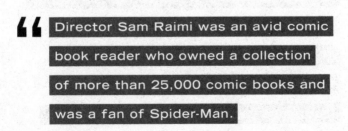

Director Sam Raimi was an avid comic book reader who owned a collection of more than 25,000 comic books and was a fan of Spider-Man.

Raimi had done some science fiction and horror films. Up to that point, the biggest film he had directed was *For Love of the Game* with an $80 million budget, and the most he had generated at the box office was $49 million worldwide for *Darkman*.[34] But he was up for the task. Again, Arad and Feige consulted with Raimi, but he hardly needed it. He started shooting the film in January of 2001 using a script that took elements from two different Marvel Spider-Man storylines. The main change he made to the character, which received a negative reaction from comic book fans, was that he has the Spider-Man portrayed by Toby McGuire shooting webs organically from his wrists as a result of the radioactive spider bite, instead of using home-made mechanical wrist guns firing a webbing invented by the teenager. When challenged by fans, Raimi explained that he thought his portrayal was more credible than having a high school boy producing, in his spare time, a wonder adhesive that even 3M could not create.[35]

When *Spider-Man* opened in April of 2002, it was a smash hit. It grossed $39 million on opening day—a new box office world record.[36] It was the first film ever to gross $100 million in its opening weekend. And in the end, it earned more than $825 million worldwide. It was a blockbuster, and suddenly everyone in Hollywood got it. They realized superhero movies could be made, they could be good, and they would make money.

Marvel's Take—Not So Marvelous

Despite the huge success of *Spider-Man*, Marvel made less money than they thought they deserved. In addition to the initial $10 million, Sony paid Marvel only $11 million more in royalties in 2002.[37] And while it was true that Marvel's toy sales rose 69 percent that year, to $155 million, Marvel had to split much of that revenue with Sony.[38]

"When we started to understand the business," said Arad, "we realized the 5 percent was pitiful and the deal on DVDs was even more insulting."[39] From that time forward Arad worked to try to get better terms, but it was difficult. At the least, he negotiated Marvel's receiving a percentage of gross revenue, rather than net profits.[40] Movie studios were notorious for using accounting that ensured that movies didn't show much profit, no matter how much money they generated.

But even more galling to Arad was the way Sony seemed to be taking credit for Spider-Man, as if Marvel was no part of the character's history. "Sony carried the banner for Spider-Man. It's our brand, but they're getting all the benefit," Arad complained.[41] Arad soon came up with a way to combat that. He asked Perlmutter for $80,000 so that he could create an animated branding piece with the Marvel logo. The Marvel Enterprises boss didn't see the point, but Arad fought for it and eventually got it.[42] That animated logo of flipping comic book pages, or an updated version of it, has appeared in every movie with a Marvel hero since Spider-Man.

> Sony carried the banner for Spider-Man. It's our brand, but they're getting all the benefit."

Marvel also sued Sony, asking for $50 million and a termination of its licensing deal. Marvel's claim was that Sony was withholding merchandising revenue and attempting to dissociate Spider-Man from the comic book company that owned him.[43]

Sony countersued, claiming Marvel was trying to get out of a sound contract.[44] In 2004, Sony settled with Marvel. The two companies didn't disclose details, but they agreed to allow Marvel to handle all licensing work for Spider-Man, whether it related to the movies or not, and they would split all merchandise revenue 75/25 percent in Marvel's favor.[45]

Finally in the Black Again

The year of *Spider-Man*'s appearance in theaters was also the year when Marvel Enterprises finally stopped losing money.[46] And those in Hollywood who hadn't already been knocking at Marvel's door before Spider-Man was a big hit, came looking to license superheroes for movies afterward. *Blade II* (New Line Cinema) came out later that year. Then the next year, superhero movies really started flowing:

2003
X2: X-Men United (Twentieth Century Fox)
Daredevil (Twentieth Century Fox)
Hulk (Universal Pictures)

2004
The Punisher (Lionsgate and Artisan)
Spider-Man 2 (Columbia Pictures)
Blade: Trinity (New Line Cinema)

2005
Elektra (Twentieth Century Fox)
Man-Thing (Lions Gate)
Fantastic Four (Twentieth Century Fox)

2006

X-Men: Last Stand (Twentieth Century Fox)

2007

Ghost Rider (Columbia Pictures)
Spider-Man 3 (Columbia Pictures)
Fantastic Four: Rise of the Silver Surfer (Twentieth Century Fox)

Plus, plenty of other films with Marvel characters in development at various studios.[47]

These superhero movies were a mixed bag. The three *X-Men* movies grossed $2 billion.[48] The three Spider-Man movies $2.5 billion.[49] *Fantastic Four* and *Daredevil* did decent business. *Hulk* made money, but it was considered a disappointment. *Elektra* and *The Punisher* were major flops."[50] *Man-Thing* cost $30 million to make and grossed less than $10 million worldwide.[51]

The breakthrough for Marvel superheroes in Hollywood during this time period was significant, but the five studios using Marvel's intellectual property were making most of the money, which frustrated Arad and Perlmutter. For example, while the X-Men made Twentieth Century Fox $2 billion, it made Marvel only $26 million—less than 2 percent.[52]

> **The breakthrough for Marvel superheroes in Hollywood during this time period was significant, but the five studios using Marvel's intellectual property were making most of the money.**

Stan Lee Searches for His Place

While Arad was working these deals, Stan Lee's role in Hollywood and at Marvel continued to diminish. He would consult on movies, trying to help directors and producers understand the characters and their worlds. And he would make cameo appearances in the movies themselves, but he wasn't at the heart of the deal making or the filmmaking.

This was frustrating Lee. He branched out and tried other things. He wrote. He created Stan Lee Media, an internet-based content company, but it failed.[53] Lee later founded POW! Entertainment in an effort to develop movie, TV, and video games of his own, separate from Marvel. It saw limited success.

In 2002, Lee sued Marvel Enterprises and Marvel Characters for $10 million,[54] stating that the 1998 deal he had negotiated with Ike Perlmutter, naming Lee chairman emeritus, paying him a generous annual salary, providing his wife with a pension, and promising him 10 percent of Marvel's movie and TV profits, wasn't being honored.[55] The *Comics Journal* said it was like Colonel Sanders suing Kentucky Fried Chicken.[56]

In 2005, Marvel Studios announced a settlement with Stan Lee. Lee received $10 million and would continue to collect his yearly salary, but it terminated Lee's rights to future profits.[57]

But then in 2007, the Stan Lee Media groups filed $1 billion in suits against Marvel Entertainment. That suit was eventually settled when in 2009 when Disney bought Marvel and agreed to a small piece of POW! Entertainment plus pay $1.25 million a year to POW! Entertainment to use Lee as a consultant.[58] That arrangement, along with his regular cameo appearances in all of Marvel's movies, held for the rest of Lee's life. He died in 2018.

Why Not Make Your Own Movies?

Arad was looking for better ways to make movies and money when Amir Malin, co-chief executive officer of Artisan, with whom Arad had made a licensing deal in 2000, asked him a question. "Why don't you finance your own pictures?" said Malin. "Why don't you collect the lion's share of the benefits from this wonderful brand you have? If you're successful, you have a multi-billion-dollar enterprise."[59]

Arad loved the idea and had a "Marvel World" plan created to present to Perlmutter. But the Marvel Entertainment CEO knew that when it came to movies, it was either feast or famine, and he had no interest in taking on the huge expenses or massive risks of making movies.[60]

While Arad was unable to convince Perlmutter to let Marvel make its own movies, someone else did. David Maisel, a graduate of Duke University and Harvard Business School, had worked with Michael Ovitz at Creative Artists Agency and Disney, then with theatrical producer Livent and Endeavor Talent Agency.[61] Maisel had been observing what was happening with Marvel and its licensing deals. He recognized that the company's focus was on licensing characters with the philosophy that the more movies that were made, the better it was because there would be more consumer products to sell.[62] But he speculated about what might happen if Marvel owned its movies. And he thought about the power of putting several of Marvel's superheroes on the screen together just as it had done in its comics for decades.[63]

Though known for his business acumen, Maisel wanted to flex his creativity. He had aspirations for becoming a producer,[64] and he knew comic books, because he was a fan.[65] Inspired by what by George Lucas had done with *Star Wars*, Maisel approached Arad to pitch the idea of Marvel making its own movies.[66] In turn, Arad introduced Maisel to Perlmutter.[67] In a meeting in Florida, Maisel claimed that he could at least negotiate a bigger share of the box-office gross than the 5 percent the company had been receiving.[68] Furthermore, he stated his desire to make it possible for Marvel to produce its own films. He proposed to do all the work and Marvel would own 100 percent of its movies.[69] Said Maisel, "The movies should be made by people who love the characters, love the stories, and really care about these movies being the best they can. People who don't just make million-dollar salaries regardless, while they're making lots of other movies."[70]

Perlmutter must have been convinced, because he hired Maisel and installed him as president and chief operating officer of the newly created Marvel Studios, reporting to CEO Avid Arad.[71] Perlmutter and Marvel's board gave him the okay to move forward, as long as Marvel wouldn't have to put up a dime.[72]

> **" Inspired by what by George Lucas had done with *Star Wars*, Maisel approached Arad to pitch the idea of Marvel making its own movies. In turn, Arad introduced Maisel to Perlmutter.**

With the support of Arad and Perlmutter, Maisel began developing a plan. He reasoned that if Marvel could put their characters onscreen without spending money, but didn't need to share merchandizing revenue, they could greatly increase profits—even if they weren't blockbusters at the box office. "If we could do movies similar to the box-office average of the [Marvel films] that had been released," figured Maisel, "or even a haircut to those, significantly, Marvel could be worth in the billions."[73]

The first thing Maisel did was ask Marvel to put a freeze on licensing deals while he figured out a plan.[74] Marvel was just about to license Captain America to Warner Bros and Thor to Sony. Maisel stopped it. "If I had gotten there three months, six months later, those deals would have been done. And there would be no chance to bring all these characters together."[75]

The next thing he did was try to prove his concept. He worked out a deal with Lionsgate to do low-budget animated Iron Man and Avengers movies that would go direct-to-DVD. Lionsgate put up 100 percent of the financing, and Marvel split the profit with them 50-50.[76] Maisel observed, "It allowed me to say to people: 'Look at the value of our IP. Here's someone paying all the money, and we have creative control and get half the profits.'"[77]

What a Deal

But he couldn't create a studio based on that model. He had to think bigger. He ended up going to Wall Street to look for the money. This was in 2005, in the wake of the economic bubble. Wall Street was looking for new investment vehicles, which made them open to his overtures. Investors were also starstruck by the prospect of working with people in Hollywood. Maisel used that to his advantage.[78]

It took Maisel a year to work out the deal he wanted. In April of 2005 Marvel announced the deal Maisel had struck. Merrill Lynch was going to provide Marvel with $525 million and allow Marvel to greenlight any movie it wanted with a budget up to $165 million, as long as the movie was rated PG-13. Marvel would put up no cash and assume no risk.[79] In addition, Marvel would keep all of the consumer product rights and 100 percent of the revenue from toy sales.[80] Marvel would retain creative control, build its film library, and keep control of its characters.[81] Maisel described the deal as "too good to be true."[82]

> " Maisel offered them collateral—not a share of Marvel. He put up Marvel's characters themselves. On the block were Ant-Man, the Avengers, Black Panther, Captain America, Doctor Strange, Hawkeye, Nick Fury, and others.

How did Maisel pull it off? Why was Merrill Lynch willing to put up the money? It was because Maisel offered them collateral—not a share of Marvel. He put up Marvel's characters themselves. On the block were Ant-Man, the Avengers, Black Panther, Captain America, Doctor Strange, Hawkeye, Nick Fury, Power Pack, and Shang-Chi, the Master of Kung Fu. Marvel could make four movies with any of those characters. If those movies failed and they failed to pay back their

loan, the movie rights for the remaining characters would belong to Merrill Lynch. But no matter what happened, Marvel
still retained merchandising revenues. And Marvel would receive 5 percent of box office gross as a service fee even if Merrill Lynch obtained the character rights and sold them to
another studio. That was what Marvel had been making in its
old licensing deals. "If [the backers] wanted to make films of
those characters, they still had to pay a service fee of 5 percent
of the gross," said Maisel. "We were no worse off than the
current situation."[83]

Arad hoped the movies would break even, Marvel would get
its 5 percent no matter what, and make a lot of money on products because they would control the timing of the movie releases and pick characters that would make great toys.[84] Maisel
believed conservatively that even product sales tied to the movies would make Marvel between $25 million and $50 million
per film. And he would get at least four tries at success before
Merrill Lynch could pull the plug.[85] However, he also said, "Our
upside, if it works, is billions."[86]

People in Hollywood considered the deal challenging and
risky for Marvel because the characters they had to use weren't
Marvel's best.[87] A writer for the *Los Angeles Times* commented,
"If you needed to launch a Hollywood franchise—are those the
superheroes you would really turn to?"[88] Maisel believed that
Marvel—and only Marvel—was capable of making good movies
with relatively minor characters because they were the only
ones who knew them well enough.[89] Arad was even more confident. "Nobody knows better than us how to make our characters come alive for audiences," he said. "We just want to get
paid for it."[90]

There was one hiccup. In the spring of 2005 as the deal was
being worked out, Merrill Lynch got cold feet. They changed

course and asked Marvel put up a third of the money for the film budgets. Marvel's board was adamant. They would not risk any of Marvel's money to make movies.

That could have killed the deal—and Marvel Studios' big opportunity. But Arad, Maisel, and Feige had been around the movie business long enough—and they were creative enough—to come up with a solution.

> If you needed to launch a Hollywood franchise—are those the superheroes you would really turn to?" Maisel believed that was capable of making good movies with relatively minor characters. Arad was even more confident: "Nobody knows better than us how to make our characters come alive for audiences."

In the United States and Canada, distribution is usually handled by one studio. But in other countries, different companies bid to handle distribution. Arad, Maisel, and Feige knew they could pre-sell foreign distribution rights to raise some cash, which is what independent filmmakers typically do to bankroll their films. So that's what they did.[91] Feige said, "I pitched that movie dozens of times to foreign buyers because we had to get . . . a large percentage of financing from selling it, pre-selling the foreign [rights]. We had a completion bond company,"[92] meaning that the money was promised, fulfilling

Merrill Lynch's requirement, but the money would not actually be paid until the film was delivered. That was enough to satisfy Merrill Lynch.

In September of 2005, financing closed,[93] and Marvel Enterprises became Marvel Entertainment. It was time for Marvel Studios to begin creating its own movies.

"Let's face it: this isn't the worst thing you've ever caught me doing."

—TONY STARK

CHAPTER FOUR

ALL
IN WITH
IRON MAN

The first question Marvel Studios' leaders had to answer was which superhero would star in their first film. Marvel's producers were in a great position. For most big movies, a studio puts up the money. That means it has control and calls the shots. But because Marvel had arranged the financing up front themselves, they could make any kind of movie they wanted about any of the heroes who were on the list of characters they had put up as collateral—as long as they followed the budget and ratings guidelines in the deal.

"I had been involved and Marvel had been involved at certain levels on other films before," said Feige, "but always as a partner, never as the lead decision maker. The other studios spent the money to make the films—they had control of the films. When we got the chance to do it ourselves, there was a lot of pressure involved, because it was all on us. But I was very comfortable with that because: If we were to fail, at least we would have failed with the best intentions."[1]

> **"** When we got the chance to do it ourselves, there was a lot of pressure involved, because it was all on us. But I was very comfortable with that because: If we were to fail, at least we would have failed with the best intentions."

Marvel needed this first movie to succeed, no matter what Maisel may have believed about getting four tries. If the first Marvel-made Marvel superhero movie was a dud, would anyone show up to see a second movie? Or would comic book fans write them off as incapable of making movies about their own heroes? Arad, Maisel, and Feige knew the stakes were high.

Arad and Maisel often disagreed about which characters to use, how much money should be slated for the budget, and how quickly to make the movies.[2] By this time, Maisel had been elevated to the position of vice chairman of Marvel Studios, but he answered directly to Perlmutter, not to Arad. This created tension between the California team of Arad and Feige, by then the president of Marvel Studios,[3] and Maisel and Perlmutter in New York.[4]

Arad's first choice as the star was Captain America, the only superstar superhero on the list.[5] But he also wanted options. Some have speculated that the strategy from the beginning was to work toward creating an Avengers film,[6] but that wasn't actually the case when they started. Feige admitted, "We had no real plans [for the Avengers] at that point. It was a pipe dream. So much of what we've done is based on a pipe dream."[7]

Arad wanted to get back the rights to Iron Man. New Line had them, but they were set to expire at the end of 2005, just months after the financing was settled with Merrill Lynch. One report stated that Arad and Maisel refused to let New Line renew the rights.[8] Another said that New Line wasn't really interested in Iron Man and let the option lapse.[9] Either way, Iron Man returned to Marvel's control.

Marvel also wanted Hulk, whose rights at that time were held by Universal Studios. There is some disagreement between Arad and Maisel about who actually made the deal to get Hulk back, but here's the gist of what happened. When the president and COO of Universal was asked whether he had plans to make another *Hulk*, he said no. When Marvel offered to let Universal Studios distribute a future film with Hulk as the main character, Universal agreed to let Marvel receive the rights back.[10] If Universal wasn't planning to make another Hulk movie, then receiving money from distribution was an unexpected bonus to them.

Who Is Our Hero?

Now they had all of the original members of the Avengers plus a few others.[11] They decided they would plan to make two films. And they had to choose who would be the star of the first one.

People who don't know Marvel's story might be shocked by how the hero of the first movie was picked, but when you're aware that Marvel has a long history of using the screen to drive product sales—whether comic books in the early years or action figures more recently—the selection process may come as no surprise. Marvel put together a focus group of children to see what toy they liked the best. They showed the kids pictures of the characters under consideration, described their abilities and weapons, and asked the children which would make the best toy that they'd most like to play with. The overwhelming answer was Iron Man.[12]

Iron Man might seem to have been an unlikely choice because he had such a long and *unsuccessful* history in Hollywood without ever getting on the big screen. The Cannon Group had bought the rights to him in the 1980s, wanting Tom Selleck to play Tony Stark and the maker of *RoboCop* to design and build the Iron Man suit.[13] In the early 1990s, Universal Pictures had the rights,[14] but they sold them to Twentieth Century Fox in 1996.[15] Fox asked Stan Lee to co-write a script, which the president of Fox liked. He said it helped him understand the character of Iron Man for the first time.[16] Nicolas Cage showed interest in playing Iron Man. So did Tom Cruise, but neither panned out. At one point, Fox approached Quentin Tarantino asking him to write and direct an Iron Man."[17] But eventually Fox stopped trying to figure out Iron Man. In 2000, they sold the rights to New Line Cinema.

Another Iron Man screenplay was written. Joss Whedon was approached to direct, then Nick Cassavetes.[18] But New Line's CEO never really bought in to the viability of Iron Man as a successful movie hero. He once told Arad, "I'll never make a movie in which Iron Man flies! It just doesn't make any sense! Steel cannot fly!"[19] In all, Iron Man spent almost two decades in development hell—only to be saved when Marvel took him back and decided to make a movie about him themselves.

Now, they decided, they would bring him to life. And for the second movie, they would feature Hulk. "We didn't have Spider-Man. We didn't have Fantastic Four," said Feige. Others said they had only B-list characters. "I never really thought that," said Feige, "because I knew that Iron Man was really cool and Hulk was, arguably, next to Spider-Man, the biggest character we had. I thought they all had amazing potential, but the goal was to deliver these two movies, and make the best *Iron Man* film we could, and make the best version of *Hulk*, even coming five years after another version of *Hulk*."[20] The Marvel producers in California let the Marvel executives in New York know that Iron Man would be their first movie. When they got the word, the East Coast team started planning the release of Iron Man toys for 2008.[21] Arad, Maisel, and Feige now had a deadline for delivering a film. The clock was ticking.

> **In all, Iron Man spent almost two decades in development hell—only to be saved when Marvel took him back and decided to make a movie about him themselves.**

An Unexpected Director

In April of 2006, Marvel hired Jon Favreau to direct *Iron Man*.[22] The choice was surprising to many because he had limited experience. He'd directed a few things for television and three movies: *Made*, a small-budget buddy comedy that Favreau wrote, directed, and starred in; *Elf*, a Christmas comedy that did well at the box office, but wasn't yet a holiday perennial; and *Zathura*, a children's movie with a $65 million budget which failed to earn back its budget with worldwide sales.[23] But Favreau impressed Arad with his knowledge of Iron Man, his ideas for updating the story, his use of comedy, and his experience using visual effects. Plus, Favreau had proven he could create energy and explore relational dynamics as he did in *Elf.* [24]

"We got to know Jon when he played Foggy in *Daredevil,*" said Arad. "I liked all the movies he directed, but I was most impressed with *Zathura.* So many of my friend's kids saw that film five or six times and I kept hearing how much they loved it. Jon is a great storyteller and smart filmmaker with a deep love and appreciation for the Marvel brand and Iron Man character. Also, to pull this film off we really needed a director who was tuned in to what was going on in the world today, both politically and socially. Jon possessed all of these characteristics."[25]

"Hiring Favreau . . . at the time was an unexpected choice," said Feige. "Going back to my experience watching Sony and Laura Ziskin and Avi hire Sam [Raimi], or Fox hire Bryan Singer, those were not people who had just come out with a big, giant blockbuster and now were doing their next. They were filmmakers who'd done super-interesting movies on a lesser scale coming into a bigger platform. I think that's always been the way we like to bring in filmmakers."[26]

Favreau saw it as a great opportunity. "I grew up reading Marvel Comics," he said. "It's an exciting challenge to direct *Iron Man* because he's the biggest character in the original pantheon of the Marvel universe who has never had a movie made about him. I come from the independent film world, and what I like to think I bring to the table is the ability to tell a story in a simple, relatable way that brings out the humor in situations, as well as the humanity of the characters. One of the great assets of Marvel Comics is that the heroes are very human and flawed. Marvel began when the iconography of the superhero was larger-than-life. They were usually flawless paradigms of integrity. But Marvel changed the landscape by creating superheroes with their own shortcomings and a recognizable humanity that is enjoyable and interesting to explore."[27]

> **Marvel began when the iconography of the superhero was larger-than-life. They were usually flawless paradigms of integrity. But Marvel changed the landscape by creating superheroes with their own shortcomings and a recognizable humanity that is enjoyable and interesting to explore."**

Favreau had a vision for what an Iron Man movie could be. He saw it as "a kind of independent film-espionage thriller crossbreed; a Robert Altman-directed *Superman,* with shades of Tom Clancy novels, James Bond films, *RoboCop,* and *Batman Begins.*"[28] He wanted to tell a great story and make it something that appealed to people who didn't know anything about Iron Man, but he felt it was important to make a movie comic book fans would love. "What the studios had done, typically, is ignore the core fans because they only represent a small fraction of the potential audience and focus on the mainstream audience," said Favreau.[29] "Time and time again, it's been proven that the studios care about making money, it's their job. They want to take the source material and use it to make it as appealing as possible to the broadest possible audience, while costing the least to make, and making the most profits."[30]

Favreau was on the same page with Feige and Arad. They wanted to bring the source material to life, but also protect it.

"I definitely feel as a fan, there's a responsibility to stay true to the expectations of the fans," said Favreau. "That doesn't always mean doing what's in the source material, but it means considering it and making decisions not because of you arbitrarily wanting to change something, but because you think it services the material the best."[31] Feige said, "We've always said we're replicating the experience of reading the comics on a big stage, and it has to work for people who read those comics and know what that experience is like, but it also needs to work for people who never opened a comic in their lives. That we know the sensation we're going to try to evoke in the audience gives us an advantage."[32]

Juggling Act

A director is like a juggler having to safely keep in the air ideas as ephemeral as cotton candy, egos as fragile as crystal vases, experts as sharp as knives, and executives who want to cut him up like chain saws—all while being a ringleader proclaiming to one and all the wonders of the show that they are about to see. During pre-production, Favreau was developing the main character, framing the story, working with script writers, envisioning the world, interacting with designers, consulting with practical and visual effects experts, and work to cast the perfect actor in every role.

Favreau knew he wanted to set the movie in California, to make it different from urban East Coast settings of most superhero stories. He wanted to base Tony Stark on Howard Hughes, just as Stan Lee had originally done when he created Iron Man. "Howard Hughes was one of the most colorful men of our time," said Lee. "He was an inventor, an adventurer, a multimillionaire, a ladies' man and, finally, a nutcase. What triggered me to create a character like Iron Man was that I wanted to do something different than the usual superhero. In 1963, Iron Man was all the things that young readers in those days didn't really care for: he was an industrialist and created war machines. I thought to myself, I'm going to make these kids like him by making Tony Stark a rich, glamorous, handsome, interesting guy."[33] And Favreau wanted to update the issues to the modern world—the original Stark got captured in Vietnam.

The script was already in progress when Favreau got hired.[34] He worked with screenwriters at every stage of the writing process, making sure their emphasis was on the people and their stories. "We really believed in having a character that was as interesting, if not more interesting, outside of the costume as he was in the costume," said Feige.[35] Favreau also brought in a group of talented Marvel comic book writers and artists to give their advice on the script.[36]

Favreau wanted the movie to look as realistic as possible. "I had a big sign that said, 'Plausibility,' and hung that sign above my door," the director remembered, "so that everybody who came in for a meeting would have to read that and remember that that was the tone of our film."[37] Favreau hired Stan Winston Studios to construct Iron Man's suit.[38] He hired Industrial Light and Magic to do the movie's digital effects after seeing their work on the *Transformers* and *Pirates of the Caribbean* movies.[39] He wanted to make the blending of practical effects—physically built props and costumes—with digital effects to create an environment and characters that looked real. Favreau even worked to get approval from the Department of Defense for the movie. "When you get DOD approval on a film," explained Feige, "you get access to lots of cool planes and vehicles and other military assets."[40]

Shifts in Leadership

While Favreau was working through the pre-production process, there was conflict between Arad and his New York counterparts. Though Maisel wanted to be known for his creativity, his primary focus was financial—as was Perlmutter's. Arad didn't like it when executives from New York wanted to weigh in on creative decisions or try to pinch pennies in the budget. New York also wanted creative decisions to be run though what came to be called the Creative Committee. It included Marvel Entertainment president Alan Fine, comic book writer Brian Michael Bendis, Marvel Comics publisher Dan Buckley, and Marvel editor in chief Joe Quesada.[41] Arad thought he had earned the right to make movies without being micromanaged or criticized.

When Arad was called a "greedy pig" for wanting to do things his own way, he was done fighting.[42] He let Perlmutter know that at the end of 2006, he would step down as chairman and CEO of Marvel Studios as well as chief creative officer of Marvel Entertainment. He would continue to consult on Marvel movies, but as an independent producer. He also cashed out most of his Marvel stock for $59 million.[43] "It was my only choice," said Arad, "because one day came when I said, 'I think I've had enough of this.' The company was growing with the CEO of this, and the CFO of that, but it was basically [a situation in which] we were doing everything but now there's way too many people for me to deal with. And everybody wanted to make movies. Everyone. I mean, you name it, the people who were cleaning the place wanted to read the scripts."[44]

With Arad's departure, Kevin Feige, who already was the most knowledgeable comic book expert among the producers, began to emerge as the driving creative force at Marvel Studios, while Maisel continued to focus primarily on the business side of things.

I Am Iron Man

Believe it or not, the first role Favreau cast was not that of Iron Man. It was of Lt. Colonel James "Rhodey" Rhodes. Wanting a high caliber actor, he cast Terrence Howard, who has been nominated for an Oscar for *Hustle & Flow*. Howard ended up receiving the highest salary of the entire cast: $3.5 million.[45]

But the most important role was that of Tony Stark. Timothy Olyphant reportedly read for the role. Hugh Jackman was high on the list of candidates.[46] So were Clive Owen and Sam Rockwell.[47] But Favreau really wanted to cast Robert Downey Jr. whose performance in *Kiss Kiss Bang Bang* impressed him.[48] More importantly, he thought Downey's life story would bring depth to the character. "The best and worst moments of Robert's life have been in the public eye," observed Favreau. "He had to find an inner balance to overcome obstacles that went far beyond his career. That's Tony Stark. Robert brings a depth that goes beyond a comic book character having trouble in high school, or can't get the girl." He also believed that Downey was so charming that he could depict a likable jerk who goes through an emotional journey that wins over the audience.[49]

Nobody else wanted Downey. Favreau said, "there was an unequivocal resounding 'no' when I presented him."[50] There were questions about his insurability because of his past addiction and erratic behavior.[51] And he was considered too old. "He's ten years older than they would have liked me to hire," said Favreau. "He's already in his forties, so I got it. They were scared of him. They told me 'no, I couldn't hire him' and it felt like too big of a risk. They wanted me to go with somebody younger and somebody with less of a reputation, and I was like, 'This could be like casting Johnny Depp in *Pirates*.' This could define the movie and bring it out of obscurity and out of this sort of 'second-rate Spider-Man' status that it's in."[52]

> " The best and worst moments of Robert's life have been in the public eye. He had to find an inner balance to overcome obstacles that went far beyond his career. That's Tony Stark. Robert brings a depth that goes beyond a comic book character having trouble in high school, or can't get the girl."

Downey desperately wanted the part. "Robert Downey Jr. wanted to play Tony Stark as much as I wanted him to play the character," recalled Favreau.[53]

"I refused to lose this part to anything or anyone. I hadn't felt that way since *Chaplin*," said Downey. "The only time I've screen-tested since *Chaplin* was for *Iron Man*."[54] (Downey filmed *Chaplin* in 1991.) Favreau said, "Sitting across from him, the lightbulb just went off over my head, and I realized this was the guy that could bring me home. This is the #1 draft pick that's going to take me to the Super Bowl. I got how to make the movie, how we were not going to just be a poor man's Spider-Man if I could get this guy."[55]

Favreau had a difficult time convincing Marvel's executives that Downey was the right person to play Iron Man. "We had a lot of people anxious about it and against it," said Favreau, "and the board was concerned and against, and then we put [Robert] on film and from the minute he opened his mouth everybody who saw the screen test was convinced, and everybody was behind him and we never looked back."[56]

"We needed a Tony Stark, and Tony Stark needed to be cool," commented Arad. "You know, Hollywood likes them to be twenty-six and cut, but Tony Stark was not a young kid. He's like a young adult that has a complexity in the story, and then we got very lucky. We ended up with Robert Downey Jr."[57]

Great casting has become a hallmark of Marvel Studios. "It's the same thought process and the same creative process," said Feige describing their mindset: "Find the best people for the part, find the best actors for the role, whether they're famous or not, whether they have marquee value or not."[58]

As *Iron Man* screenwriter Mark Fergus commented, "It's a slightly off-beat choice, but Marvel has a cool and visionary way of casting its films. When the casting is announced, people usually react with, 'oh that's interesting,' and then it turns out to be more than interesting. It turns out to be perfect and people can't imagine anybody else in the role. Marvel's really adventurous like that and I think that audiences really appreciate it."[59]

"Why am I the guy for this job?" Downey explained. "Because the story is the most duplicitous and conflicted of all the Marvel characters, because he's really just a guy who gets put in an extraordinary set of circumstances—partially due to his own character defects and partially due to his lineage—and you can pick a . . . million Joseph Campbell myths and look 'em up, but none of them apply more to me, and there's nothing I could bring more to than this job and this story."[60]

With Downey, Favreau had the most important piece for the *Iron Man* puzzle. "The hardest and most important challenge that I faced was getting Robert approved," said Favreau, "and once Robert was cast, everything else was much easier relative to that because I knew I was going to have a good movie," said Favreau.

As soon as Downey was cast, he set up an office next to Favreau's to discuss his role and to be involved in the writing of the film.[61] "When Robert Downey Jr. came on board he became a true partner creatively," said Favreau.[62]

Shooting . . . Sometimes from the Hip

Filming began in March of 2007, and it was still a juggling act, because the script wasn't completely finished. "Well, these movies don't really have scripts which are locked in a traditional sense," explained Favreau. A "locked" script isn't supposed to change. "I mean it's sort of the dirty secret about these superhero films is the script is unfortunately the last thing to get the proper attention. It's part of the logistics of the process. You're chasing a date, you're chasing effects, your priorities are in different areas, and you have writers working to try to conform to this larger story that you are telling. As a director, you understand the story, but from a writing perspective, the script usually isn't caught up yet to where the story has evolved to through storyboards, so you hit the set understanding what the scene is about, but how you get there is achieved in different ways."[63]

Favreau said that most of the dialogue in the film was ad-libbed, making the interaction between the characters feel more natural. He shot some scenes with two cameras instead of one. That made it possible to capture both actors as they improvised dialog that would be difficult to duplicate for a second camera setup. Downey was fantastic at this kind of improvisation and would ask to do multiple takes of a scene to try new ideas. Not everyone thrived in that kind of environment. Gwyneth Paltrow had a hard time keeping up.[64] And Jeff Bridges, a consummate professional, said he was uncomfortable since he was used to doing his lines word-perfect from memory. But he adjusted after he started to think of *Iron Man* as a "two hundred million dollar student film."[65] But Favreau was an expert at developing a collaborative creative environment, which helped. As Feige said, "When you combine Robert's acting ability with the adventure and spectacle of the comic book genre, you end up with something that is bigger than the sum of its parts."[66]

Mixed Expectations

As *Iron Man* finished filming and went into post-production, Marvel worked to build anticipation for the film and get the word out about it. Because they had stayed true to the source material, they were able to start with the comic book fans. "I think the challenge has been first people getting to know who Iron Man was, and I think that the online fans and the fanbase did a tremendous service to me and the film by bringing it to everybody's attention," said Favreau at the time. "And when they saw the footage at Comic-Con and saw all the online leaks, either the ones we sent out there with releases or ones that found their way through spies. People started to get Iron Man, to anticipate it, and the word started to spread, and it worked its way into the mainstream and now everybody wants to see the movie."[67]

From the beginning, the Marvel executives in New York hadn't expected this first film to be highly successful. Back when Downey was cast, a Marvel board member told Maisel, "Don't worry. We'll be very happy if this breaks even and we can sell more toys."[68] But even toy sales were in jeopardy as the release date approached. Marvel couldn't convince toy manufacturers to get on board for *Iron Man*.[69] Compared to the $285 million budget of *Spider-Man 3*, which was produced around the same time, *Iron Man*'s $140 million budget looked small. On top of that, toy manufacturers didn't think of Iron Man as an A-list character, the actor cast in the title role was talented but questionable, and the studio was unproven. "We couldn't give Iron Man away, nobody wanted it," said one Marvel executive. "So there was not very much merchandise on the shelves for the first movie."[70]

> Compared to the $285 million budget of *Spider-Man 3*, *Iron Man*'s $140 million budget looked small. On top of that, toy manufacturers didn't think of Iron Man as an A-list character, the actor cast in the title role was talented but questionable, and the studio was unproven.

Initial projections for the total U.S. box office of *Iron Man* were around $100 million.[71] With toy sale revenue limited and a domestic box office that wouldn't break even, Marvel executives were worried. They might need overseas movie sales to make any kind of profit.

The Payoff

When *Iron Man* opened, it made $99 million—in one weekend, almost reaching the lifetime expected revenue from U.S. sales. At that time, it was the second-highest opening weekend for a non-sequel in the United States. The record was held by another Marvel superhero movie: *Spider-Man*.[72] It wasn't until after that weekend that Feige realized they would be able to make more Marvel movies.[73] And because Feige had thought of shooting a short scene with Samuel L. Jackson as Nick Fury interacting with Iron Man and inserting it after the credits as an Easter egg for comic book fans, he also realized that the films they made could be linked together.[74]

In the end, *Iron Man* grossed $585M worldwide and generated more than $100 million in profits. It drove an increase of 22 percent in Iron Man comic sales. Marvel's total revenue was increased by nearly 40 percent in 2008 to $676 million.[75] And the toy manufacturers quickly jumped on board, with Iron Man performing as a perennial best-seller. Iron Man action figures by Hasbro earned $18.7 million in global retail sales between 2011–2016.[76]

In the wake of *Iron Man*'s success, Favreau said, "It was wonderful but also disorienting. Everything shifts. Everything changes a bit for everybody. It's like a band that puts out a hit song. You go from playing in a garage to trying to figure out how you're going to follow it up."[77] Favreau followed it up by agreeing to direct *Iron Man 2*, which prompted Marvel's stock to jump 9 percent the day it was announced,[78] and become a producer on six more Marvel films.[79] He also created much of the blueprint that has made Marvel movies so successful. "We ended up landing a tone with *Iron Man* that became the formula moving forward," said Favreau. "You want to mix great casting, stay true to the characters, a combined universe that would allow cross-pollination. And having humor and adherence to canon."[80]

> **We ended up landing a tone with *Iron Man* that became the formula moving forward. You want to mix great casting, stay true to the characters, a combined universe that would allow cross-pollination. And having humor and adherence to canon."**

Unfortunately, Marvel's producers hadn't yet learned that lesson when they were making *The Incredible Hulk* at the same time they were finishing up *Iron Man*. *The Incredible Hulk*'s director, Louis Leterrier, had a vision for the film that was dark. Edward Norton, the actor cast as Hulk, thought it should be even darker. Norton got the okay to rewrite much of the screenplay. He even wanted to open the film with a suicide attempt by the main character. But when shooting was done and *The Incredible Hulk* was being edited, Feige took over editing and removed that scene, along with many others that he believed were too negative.[81]

The film was released only a few months after *Iron Man*. The response was tepid. One reviewer called it "a forgettable detour."[82] The film review site Rotten Tomatoes gives it a score of 67 percent compared to *Iron Man*'s 93 percent.[83] In the end, *The Incredible Hulk* barely broke even, grossing $263 million worldwide. This is considered the worst performance of any Marvel Studios movie.[84] It's probably fair to say that Kevin Feige and the others learned a lot about what *not* to do in future Marvel movies.

If *The Incredible Hulk* had been released first, it might have ruined Marvel. Fortunately, it wasn't, and it didn't. It also didn't stop one of the biggest and most storied players in the movie world from knocking at their door to buy them.

"Anybody on our side hiding any shocking and fantastic abilities they'd like to disclose? I'm open to suggestions."

—TONY STARK

CHAPTER FIVE

THE EVER-EXPANDING MARVEL CINEMATIC UNIVERSE

O ver the years, there was a lot of talk about Marvel in rela-
tion to Disney. Stan Lee moved out to California because he
wanted to make Marvel the *next* Disney.[1] When New Line bought
Marvel, they wanted to open retail stores to be *like* Disney. And
observers thought that if the comic book company had been
willing to put up their own money to make movies, Marvel
could have become a strong *competitor* to Disney.[2] But in the
end, they became a *part* of Disney.

That process began in February of 2009 when Bob Iger, Disney's CEO, unexpectedly brought up the idea of purchasing
Marvel to David Maisel during a meeting between them. Over
the course of three months, Disney and Marvel negotiated, often by phone, plus in several face-to-face meetings between executives, until they landed a deal acceptable to both sides.
Disney would buy Marvel Entertainment for $4 billion in cash

and stock. They would pay $50 per share for Marvel, who tried to negotiate an even higher price. Experts stated that Disney had paid a 29 percent premium.

"Marvel's brand and its treasure trove of content will now benefit from our extraordinary reach," said Iger after the announcement. "We paid a price that reflects the value they've created and the value we can create as one company. It's a full price, but a fair price."[3]

The deal closed on December 31, 2009.[4] For the first time in its history, Marvel would have enough money to create movies the way Stan Lee, Avi Arad, and Kevin Feige had wanted. However, the path ahead wasn't completely clear. It was complicated by the shortsighted licensing deals that had been made in previous years. Disney was now entangled with Sony Pictures Entertainment, Paramount Pictures, and Twentieth Century Fox because of long-term deals Marvel had made in the past. Sony still owned the rights to Spider-Man. Paramount had an agreement to distribute five Marvel films, but in October of 2010, Disney resolved this by agreeing to pay Paramount $115 million for the worldwide distribution rights to *Iron Man 3* and *The Avengers*.[5] As part of the deal, Paramount would retain an onscreen production credit and be mentioned in marketing materials, even though films were solely owned, distributed, financed, and marketed by Disney.[6] The issue with Fox was more difficult to solve. Fox had *X-Men* and *The Fantastic Four* locked up pretty much forever.[7] It would take time for Disney to come up with a plan to deal with this problem.

Will This Really Work?

Through the transition, Kevin Feige and the rest of the producers at Marvel stayed focused. While big studios like Disney often juggled dozens or even hundreds of movie ideas, scripts, and projects in development, Marvel worked on only a few at one time, and every single one of Marvel's projects was intended to become a movie.[8] In addition, with Disney's acquisition of Marvel, it created a separate Marvel Television division, which Feige didn't have to run. That division's first offering was *Marvel's Agents of S.H.I.E.L.D.*, created by *The Avengers* director Joss Whedon and broadcast by ABC. Since then, the television division has produced Marvel shows on ABC, Netflix, Hulu, and Freeform, expanding Marvel's reach.

In the movie world, Feige was benefitting from the assistance of two Hollywood veterans who handled the heavy load of filmmaking details, keeping Feige free to be creative: Louis D'Esposito and Victoria Alonso. D'Esposito had worked his way up the ranks in Hollywood as an assistant director, the person who handles just about everyone and everything on set except for the actors and cinematographer. After serving as an executive producer and a unit production manager on *Zathura*, with Jon Favreau, D'Esposito was hired to fulfill those same roles on *Iron Man 2*. Later, he was hired full-time by Marvel and became the co-president of Marvel Studios.

Alonso's background was in visual effects. Hired as a visual effects producer on *Iron Man*, she also functioned as a co-producer. She was hired back for *Iron Man 2*, then officially brought on board at Marvel. She now serves as the executive vice president of production for Marvel Studios.

As co-president, D'Esposito typically works behind the scenes. Alonso is responsible for vision effects on all Marvel movies, but she also speaks to the press, participates in panels, and speaks to fans. About the arrangement, D'Esposito said, "I'll be fielding more of the phone calls from agents concerning deals on actors, writers, directors, etc. Victoria will lean toward delivery and post-production. Kevin is obviously everything creative."[9]

Feige and his team wanted to keep building the Marvel Cinematic Universe by completing four more films, which would come to be called Phase One: *Iron Man 2, Thor, Captain America: The First Avenger,* and *The Avengers.* The characters in these films, including Hulk from the second film, would share the same world, just as the Marvel comic book characters had from the very beginning. And the superheroes would appear in one another's stories, just as Namor and the Human Torch had way back in 1940. At Marvel Studios, that crossover had started at the end of the very first film, *Iron Man,* with the appearance of Nick Fury, played by Samuel L. Jackson, after the credits. It was initially meant to be only an Easter egg, a treat for comic book fans. "We put it at the end so it wouldn't be distracting," said Feige. But the acceptance of Fury by fans and the buzz it created confirmed Feige's instinct that the interconnection of movies would work.[10] Feige later said, "I would like to take *all* of the comics and start to build the Marvel universe."[11] With an eye toward making those connections, Marvel signed Samuel L. Jackson to a nine-picture deal.[12] He would become an important link between nearly all of the movies.

Jon Favreau signed on to direct *Iron Man 2* right after the first film debuted. Robert Downey Jr. was, of course, on board. Together, he and Favreau had helped create the template for Marvel movies. Just like *Iron Man,* each movie would be a good story, incorporating humor as well as action. The superheroes would not be one-dimensional cardboard cutouts. Instead, the stories featured flawed, multilayered characters who fought not just against injustice or evil or villains, but also against their inner conflicts or one another. While the movies were based on comic books, the relationships between the characters were given even more depth and heart. All the films were interconnected, but each also stood on its own, and they were made with a desire for excellence. "That's what we focus on," said Feige, "what we can control, which is the quality of the pictures."[13]

> **"** Just like *Iron Man*, each movie would be a good story, incorporating humor as well as action. The superheroes would not be one-dimensional cardboard cutouts. Instead, the stories featured flawed, multilayered characters who fought not just against injustice or evil or villains, but also against their inner conflicts or one another.

Providing the heart and lifeblood for each film was its director. Feige and Arad had made a fantastic choice in Jon Favreau for *Iron Man*. They had done less well with Louis Leterrier for *The Incredible Hulk*. But they had learned. "Early on, we realized that the role of the filmmaker on our films is to bring a unique tonality and be able to maintain and ride that tone over the course of production and through post-production," said Feige. "We have amazing artists and technicians who can help with the scale, that can help with as big a canvas as it is. What the film-makers need to do is not get lost in all of that and to focus on the great character work."[14]

Feige wanted every movie that Marvel produced to be unique, just like the comic books they were based on. He said, "People think (a superhero movie) means, Oh, yes, you run into a phone booth, you put on a cape, and you stop a bank robbery." In comic books, the characters and plots can be just as diverse as those in a novel. Feige noted that viewers don't tend to be as prejudiced against films made from novels, "because people inherently understand, Oh, well, that's what a novel is. All novels are different." Marvel Studios movies would demonstrate that, likewise, "all comics are different. The storylines are different. What the characters go through is different."[15]

The Marvel Method of Choosing Directors

Feige developed a method for choosing directors. In Holly-wood, directors are often courted like reluctant prom dates. They have to be convinced by their agents or the hiring pro-ducer to take the gig. At Marvel, Feige turned the tables. He and his team want directors to audition for the job. The Marvel team starts with an idea of what they want, whether in plot or tone, before they look for potential directors. Then, Feige ex-plained, "It really comes down to numerous meetings . . . where we sort of pitch what we think the movie could be [to possible directors], and then we start a discussion," through several sep-arate meetings. If, he said, the directing candidate makes it "way better than what we initially were spewing to them, they usually get the job."[16]

Even before Favreau started production on *Iron Man 2*, Feige was working to figure out *Thor*, the next Marvel superhero movie. When asked if it would be difficult to meld the fantasy of *Thor* with the high-tech science fiction of the world Iron Man and the Hulk inhabited, Feige responded, "No because we're doing the Jack Kirby/Stan Lee/Walt Simonson/J. Michael Straczynski *Thor*. We're not doing the blow-the-dust-off-of-the-old-Norse-book-in-your-library *Thor*. And in the *Thor* of the Marvel Universe, there's a race called the Asgardians."[17] In other words, Thor and his people would not be portrayed as gods from Earth. They were instead aliens from another planet. To handle their introduction, Feige hired Shakespearean actor and director Kenneth Branagh.

> When asked if it would be difficult to meld the fantasy of *Thor* with the high-tech science fiction of the world Iron Man and the Hulk inhabited, Feige responded, "No because we're doing the Jack Kirby/Stan Lee/Walt Simonson/J. Michael Straczynski *Thor*. We're not doing the blow-the-dust-off-of-the-old-Norse-book-in-your-library *Thor*. And in the *Thor* of the Marvel Universe, there's a race called the Asgardians."

A *Thor* comic book fan from his youth, Branagh wanted to create "an archetypal and mythic ideal: the great walking amongst the common." Branagh explained, "There's a coming-of-age story, a prodigal-son story, the journey from arrogance to humility. That classical structure for me means a timeless and invisible connection between the contemporary and the traditional."[18] Branagh worked for two years with the screenwriters to get the story where he wanted it. "This new dimension . . . the space adventure needed to find its starting place," he explained. "There was real concern around that. They felt that if they didn't get that one right, it was going to be really, really difficult for the expansion of that tone across the rest of what they planned."[19] And when it came time to cast *Thor*, Branagh's choices of Chris Hemsworth and Tom Hiddleston were considered "no-names." One entertainment reporter commented on the choice, "Let's hope they follow the J.J. Abrams route and put the money they saved in casting straight into special effects."[20]

While *Thor* didn't skimp on special effects, there was no need to worry about how the perfectly cast actors performed. Or the movie. While it didn't make as much as the 2010 *Iron Man 2*, whose earnings totaled nearly $624 million,[21] *Thor*, released in 2011, made $449 million worldwide.[22] That was more than the total of $370 million that *Captain America: The First Avenger*, directed by Joe Johnston, would make when it released a few months later.[23]

Something that became the norm for a Marvel film during Phase One was the inclusion of an origin story for the central character. Tony Stark's origin story was central to *Iron Man*. While Thor's wasn't a typical origin story, because he didn't suddenly receive powers or abilities like the other Marvel superheroes, *Thor* showed how the character *regained* his powers and found his place in the world. Without seeing this aspect of Thor's origin, audiences wouldn't have understood him or his motivations in later films.

The exception, however, was *The Incredible Hulk.* Feige hadn't wanted to tell the origin story again, believing that the audience had already seen it in Ang Lee's film a few years before.[24] Director Louis Leterrier and main actor Edward Norton agreed and instead recapped Hulk's origin in their movie through a short montage during the opening credits. But Feige and Marvel learned from this mistake. And since then, every Marvel movie featuring a new character has devoted more time to his or her origin story. Favreau said, "That's the Faustian deal with the first movie. You gotta show the origin story, so every first movie is two movies: the origin and then what happens with the water system of Gotham City," he said, speaking metaphorically. "They're always going to have that Frankenstein feel of being two movies."[25]

> **" That's the Faustian deal with the first movie. You gotta show the origin story, so every first movie is two movies: the origin and then what happens."**

Avengers, Assemble!

As the first five movies by Marvel Studios were being made, everything Feige and company were doing was building toward the final film of Phase One: *The Avengers.* Feige asked director Joss Whedon, who had previously worked as a script doctor on

X-Men and as a consultant on *Captain America: The First Avenger*, to consider directing *The Avengers*.[26] So Whedon wrote a five-page treatment for the film with the tagline "Avengers: Some Assembly Required." Feige liked it so much that they hired Whedon to direct and gave him only three stipulations: the Avengers had to fight against Loki; there had to be a battle among the Avengers near the middle of the movie, and, in the final battle, the Avengers had to work together to win.[27]

Whedon found that appealing. "These guys just don't belong together," he commented, noting that the characters all had different motivations, backgrounds, and issues.[28] When describing their dynamics, Whedon referenced *The Dirty Dozen*, *Dr. Strangelove*, *The Abyss*, *His Girl Friday*, and *Black Hawk Down*.[29] Feige expressed interest in how Hulk, in particular, might solve problems as an "unpredictable part" of an ensemble.[30]

As *The Avengers* was being cast, Mark Ruffalo, who had been considered to play Hulk in the original 2008 movie, was now chosen for the role. He was excited, because the animation for his character would be much different from in the past. He said, "No one's ever played the Hulk exactly; they've always done CGI." But for *The Avengers*, the Hulk would be created using stop-motion capture like what James Cameron had used in his 2009 film *Avatar*. Ruffalo enthused, "I'll actually play the Hulk. That'll be fun."[31] It was also effective.

During the shooting of the film, the cast members really came together, with Robert Downey Jr. as the ringleader and everyone's mentor. D'Esposito observed about Downey, "Watching him on set is amazing because he really understands the story. He likes to ad-lib, and he's always on point. He's always serving the story. Even when he's taking some liberties with the script, he's always making it even better." He continued, "He's like the Godfather on set, taking care of everyone."[32] Downey even insisted that Gwyneth Paltrow be brought in to play Pepper Potts on the film. Whedon hadn't intended to include supporting characters from other individual films, but he relented.[33] Jeremy Renner, who played Hawkeye, summed up how everyone felt: "The bond of the Avengers essentially is really strong on camera and off camera."[34]

> **"** Watching him on set is amazing because he really understands the story. He likes to ad-lib, and he's always on point. He's always serving the story. Even when he's taking some liberties with the script, he's always making it even better. . . . He's like the Godfather on set, taking care of everyone."

When *The Avengers* debuted, it broke the domestic box office record for an opening weekend, bringing in more than $200 million.[35] The Marvel team was pleased. But they also watched for other evidence of success. Favreau, who had served as an executive producer, commented, "You want a movie that doesn't drop off, so the number that I'm really looking forward to seeing [is next weekend's gross]." He believed later box office numbers would show whether they could maintain their audience. He explained, "That tells you that the movie's good. And this is just speaking as a director, as somebody who wants to learn if I've done the right thing and if the people out there are appreciating what I'm doing."[36] The next weekend, *The Avengers* earned more than $150 million.

Still, Kevin Feige emphasized that he didn't measure success in dollars. He said, "It's not about the tracking—other people can worry about that, later in the process. We work on: how will the audience respond?"[37] He cared about whether moviegoers enjoyed the movie. And obviously, they did. A review in *Rolling Stone* communicated the usual response. The reviewer wrote that *The Avengers* was "the blockbuster I saw in my head when I imagined a movie that brought together the idols of the Marvel world in one shiny, stupendously exciting package." He continued, "It's *Transformers* with a brain, a heart and a working sense of humor."[38]

Feige and company were definitely on track. Ultimately, the movie excited audiences worldwide, and earned $1.5 *billion*.[39] What would they do as an encore?

Marvel's Phase Two: Superheroes with a Twist

For the next phase in the Marvel Cinematic Universe's canon, Kevin Feige planned six more movies. He believed two per year was all that Marvel Studios could handle and still maintain the quality they had striven to uphold from the beginning. And after *The Avengers*, he was confident. When asked if there was a moment when he realized that the massive on-screen universe he was constructing was going to work, Feige said that *The Avengers* "taught us that the audience really gets what we're doing, and really enjoys the cross-pollination of all the different film series. And the audience told us unequivocally they were with us. That allowed us to plot out everything that we've done since then."[40]

Marvel would build on what had been introduced in the first phase, with plans for *Iron Man 3, Thor: The Dark World*, and *Captain*

America: The Winter Soldier. "As we were entering Phase Two," Kevin Feige said, "the idea was to continue what we had done in Phase One—which was not just telling new stories with those same characters, but making the same kind of choices with regards to cast and filmmakers." That included looking to hire directors who "hadn't necessarily done 'giant movies' before, but had a unique point of view and a unique angle on the world."[41]

At the same time, Kevin Feige began to think about adding some innovative elements to the Phase Two films. "I think in general, the tone of all of our movies are equal parts very serious and very lovingly respectful, and at the same time humorous," said Feige, "because that's the kind of movies we want to go see, and that's the kind of movie we want to make."[42] But he didn't want to stop there. He thought about stereotypical genre film—movies that fit into neat categories like thrillers or cop movies or romantic comedies. Perhaps if Marvel could incorporate tropes from some classic genres, it would make their superhero movies even more fun and interesting.

Feige started right away, with ideas for *Captain American: The Winter Soldier.* He told the potential directors, comic book fan brothers, Joe and Anthony Russo, his desire to make it as a genre film, "a sort of '70s political thriller." Feige described the conversations that followed, "That's what I pitched to them, and they lost their minds. They just started coming back and coming back and coming back with great ideas and great ideas and great ideas."[43]

"Reference videos, storyboards, script pages, you name it," said Joe Russo about their pitch back to Feige. "We did like a thirty-page book that had everything that we'd do with the character, from the theme of the movie to the tone of the film to the fighting style." Russo also wanted to think differently about the character because, he said, "frankly he was not one of my favorite characters growing up, I always found him a little square. So we wanted to add an element of deconstruction to the character and to examine him in a way that was different . . . to make him really flawed and human—or as flawed and human as we could."[44]

For the fourth film of Phase Two, Feige considered yet another genre: "I always wanted to do a space movie . . . a franchise set in outer space." *Guardians of the Galaxy* would certainly fit the bill. Plus, Feige said he "*loved* telling people that we were going to do this movie, *Guardians of the Galaxy*, with a raccoon and a tree," because their reaction was always so funny.[45] For a director, he was considering James Gunn, who sealed the deal when brought in a new outline, "The cover of which," said Feige, "had a picture of the very first Sony Walkman. With no explanation." Feige immediately saw how it might work, because "we knew we wanted Peter Quill to have a connection to Earth in a way that most intergalactic outer space heroes don't have. When I saw that Walkman I thought, 'he's going to do it through music,' which is genius."[46] Many would argue that the entire movie works because of the way James Gunn handled the soundtrack. That and the casting.

"I never thought we'd find the right guy," said Gunn about the screen-testing process. But he said he knew "within a minute of his test that Chris [Pratt] was Star-Lord." As for the other main characters, Gunn cast Michael Rooker as Yondu. The two men knew each other well, and Rooker had acted in all of Gunn's previous movies. He believed Rooker would bring something exciting to this role as well. As for Benicio del Toro, Glenn Close, and John C. Reilly, Gunn said they were "some of my favorite actors in the world, and we were fortunate enough to get them to agree to do this insane film."[47]

The character of Ant-Man had been one of the original Avengers in the comic books under Stan Lee's leadership.

THE EVER-EXPANDING MARVEL CINEMATIC UNIVERSE ▪ 95

Feige envisioned *Ant-Man* as an origin film, like *Iron Man, Captain America*, and *Guardians of the Galaxy,* with all the usual Marvel elements of humor, action, and heart. It would be a genre film as well. Feige wanted it to be a "heist" movie. "We make a lot of superhero movies here at Marvel Studios and I believe the key is to make them all different and to make them all unique and to make them all stand apart while connecting together," he said.[48]

Genre films offered the opportunity to showcase the differences between them, "on a much bigger canvas." Feige explained, "So we do say, We want to make a space movie. We want to do a high school movie. We want to do a heist movie. We want to do a thriller. That is how we think about all our different films. What kind of films do we want to make?"[49]

The movie rounding out Phase Two would bring all the major stars of the Marvel world back together again: *Avengers: Age of Ultron.* Its director, Joss Whedon, working with Marvel again, observed, "The cast—they were very trusting the first time around. But this time, [there's an] ease and rapport, and just the fun that we have. Everybody's got franchises and babies. Everyone's very comfortable with themselves."[50] The cast members were happy to all be together again. It was like a family reunion—only without all the dysfunction. Talking about Chris Hemsworth, Chris Evans remarked, "We're buddies. We've been on a little bit of a ride doing these movies. You make really good friendships. It sounds cliché to say: 'We all get along so well!' We *really* get along phenomenally well. It's like summer camp."[51]

"The *Avengers* films, ideally, in the grand plan are always big, giant linchpins," said Feige. "It's like as it was in publishing, when each of the characters would go on their own adventures and then occasionally team up for a big, 12-issue mega-event." The comic book characters always returned to their own stories changed in some way. Feige said, "I envision the same thing occurring after this movie, because the roster is altered by the finale of this film."[52]

" You make really good friendships. It sounds cliché to say: 'We all get along so well!' We *really* get along phenomenally well. It's like summer camp."

By the time Marvel brought Phase Two to a close, Feige and company really knew what they were doing. They had fine-tuned their planning. Periodically, he and his team went on a retreat to discuss the coming movies. "We have every few years," said Feige about how they come up with ideas. "Often it's collections of things from the comics, of course."[53] But they also remained flexible. "We always had contingency plans," explained Feige. They would ask themselves questions: "Are we going to be able to make another movie with this actor? If so, we're going to do this. If not, we're going to do this. If we get the rights to a certain character, that'd be great, we'll do this. If not, we're going to do this."[54]

Marvel had also gotten really good at picking key writers and directors. And the people they chose understood what they were getting into, working within the Marvel system. Feige observed that these directors understood "the notion of the shared sandbox more than the initial filmmakers did because [in the beginning] the sandbox didn't exist."[55]

After these six films had been released, Marvel's Phase Two came to a close. All told, they earned $5.25 billion. Feige said that success gave them even greater confidence. "The studio's firing on all cylinders right now. We have the absolute best team in Hollywood in front of the camera and behind the camera working on these movies." The biggest thing the success of the second phase did for Marvel Studios was make them comfortable with the idea of making three films a year instead of just two "without changing our methods," which was very important, according to Feige.[56]

Another Kind of Phase Two

Around the same time that the movies' Phase Two was coming to a close, leadership challenges that Kevin Feige had been dealing with for years within Marvel Studios were coming to a head. Back when Marvel Entertainment was purchased by Disney in 2009, a lot of their biggest fans were worried that Disney would start interfering too much. This was in spite of how Disney had handled their purchase of Pixar in 2006. The three features developed and produced entirely after that purchase— *Wall-E*, *Up*, and *Toy Story 3*—were all critically acclaimed and financially successful, earning $521 million,[57] $735 million,[58] and $1 billion[59] respectively. Disney followed the Pixar model with Marvel. So it wasn't Disney that complicated Marvel's moviemaking and frustrated Feige. It was Marvel's own Creative Committee, along with Ike Perlmutter, back in New York.

Just as they had with Arad, the New York Creative Committee continually meddled with the Hollywood creative process. They wanted to give notes on every project, but were often late delivering them, slowing down the development process. Furthermore, the filmmakers found the notes unhelpful. Some said the meddling had driven away two directors from Marvel projects during Phase Two and made things difficult for two more.[60] In addition, Perlmutter was rumored to have "clung to outdated opinions about casting, budgeting, and merchandising that ran counter to trends in popular culture." For example, Perlmutter had blocked the production of Black Widow-themed merchandise when the original *Avengers* was released. Some believed it was he thought "girl" superhero products wouldn't sell.[61] There was even a claim that when Don Cheadle was cast in place of Terrence Howard for the role of Rhodey in *Iron Man 2*, Perlmutter had said no one would notice the change because the actors were black.[62]

Evidently the last straw for Feige was Perlmutter's attempt to scale down the budget of the *Captain America: Civil War*, the third movie in the successful film series.[63] This prompted Feige to talk to the executives at Disney about making changes to the organizational structure. As one insider stated, "New York had a big say for a long time, but hasn't Kevin earned the right to some autonomy? He's made the company billions. Why is he reporting to a seventy-two-year-old man who doesn't make movies?"[64]

> **New York had a big say for a long time, but hasn't Kevin earned the right to some autonomy? He's made the company billions. Why is he reporting to a seventy-two-year-old man who doesn't make movies?"**

In August of 2015, the change became official. Disney announced, "Marvel Studios is taking the next logical step in its integration with The Walt Disney Studios, joining Pixar and Lucasfilm in centralizing many of its film-related functions in Burbank, with Marvel Studios president Kevin Feige and co-president Louis D'Esposito continuing to lead the Marvel Studios team reporting to Walt Disney Studios Chairman Alan Horn."[65] Perlmutter was removed from any involvement in Marvel's movies.[66]

With his team in place, the financial backing and confidence from Disney, a proven method for making movies, a fantastic track record, and the kibitzers from New York out of the way, Kevin Feige was ready to tackle the most ambitious lineup of his career: the nine movies planned for Phase Three.

CONCLUSION

I n the history of Marvel, the company had always been at its best when the businesspeople took care of the business side of things, and the writers, artist, and creative overseers possessed the freedom to be creative and do what they did best. That was true when Martin Goodman stayed on the financial side, tracking sales and measuring profits, while allowing Stan Lee to write, edit, and work with the artists to create the heroes and stories that comic book readers love, even today. Now Kevin Feige was finally in a position of creative freedom as he began to approach the creation of the movies that would comprise Marvel's Phase Three. Feige's plan was to create nine films, beginning with *Captain America: Civil War*. But a funny thing happened around that same time, and it was instigated by Ike Perlmutter.

> " Marvel has always been at its best when the businesspeople took care of the business side of things, and the writers, artist, and creative overseers possessed the freedom to be creative and do what they did best.

Homecoming

Sony's Columbia Pictures division had been in control of the movie rights for Spider-Man for more than a decade and had done well with it. *Spider-Man* and its two sequels, directed by Sam Raimi, broke box office records at the time, earning a total of $2.5 billion.[1] Feige had been part of the team who produced them, along with Avi Arad. But when Raimi bowed out of directing another sequel, Sony wasn't sure what to do. Their deal with Marvel stipulated that there could be a gap of no longer than five years and nine months between Spider-Man films, or Sony would lose the rights.[2]

Ultimately, Sony decided to do a reboot of the series. They recast Spider-Man and went forward almost as if the original three films didn't exist, telling Spider-Man's origin story again in a surprisingly similar way. That was a choice fans didn't like. *The Amazing Spider-Man* was released in 2012, but it made less than any of the other three movies. Sony followed that in 2014 with *The Amazing Spider-Man 2*. However, even with a larger budget of $260 million, it made less than expected: $708 million.[3] While that may sound like a lot of money, the film reputedly made only $20 million in profits.[4]

As Sony's Spider-Man movies failed to perform as expected, the same could be said for the Spider-Man toys and merchandize Marvel sold. That irked Perlmutter, so he began making overtures to try to get Spider-Man's rights back. Sony was not about to let that happen. Feige had another idea. He wanted to share Spider-Man with Sony. He wanted to put the character, newly cast and reintroduced, into *Captain America: Civil War*. In return, he would let Sony use Iron Man in a new Spider-Man movie produced by Columbia Pictures.

Feige approached Amy Pascal, the chairman of Sony's motion picture group, with this idea since he had worked with her before, but she rejected the idea out of hand. However, Sony later warmed to the idea, and Perlmutter tried to hammer out a deal with them, but he wanted the deal to favor Marvel too heavily. In the end, Feige and Pascal were able to work it out where Marvel made Sony's Spider-Man movie, with Sony handling the marketing and keeping all of the profits, but Marvel got 100 percent of the revenue from toys and other merchandise.[5] Hollywood observers called the deal "unusual because little money changed hands" and "the companies are sharing their most popular characters."[6]

> Spider-Man was not created in a vacuum in a world without superheroes; Spider-Man was never the only superhero in his universe. He was part of the Marvel universe. He grew up in a world where Iron Man would fly over his head and Hulk would smash cars in the streets. We'd never seen that version of Peter Parker on screen before."

"I was lucky enough to be involved on the Sam Raimi Spider-Man films," said Feige. "When it came time that Sony was talking about additional Spider-Man films, it was really gracious of Amy Pascal to hear me out when I suggested incorporating him

into the MCU. Having Spider-Man on set those early days of
Civil War, and then doing an MCU Spider-Man film, with Tony
Stark as his mentor, and tapping into a Spider-Man that nobody
had seen before outside of the comic books. . . . Spider-Man was
not created in a vacuum in a world without superheroes;
Spider-Man was never the only superhero in his universe. He
was part of the Marvel universe. He grew up in a world where
Iron Man would fly over his head and Hulk would smash cars
in the streets. We'd never seen that version of Peter Parker on
screen before."[7]

Can Sequels Ever Be More Successful Than the Originals?

With the Sony deal settled, Feige set out to build on his previous accomplishments in Phase Two. That was not going to be
an easy task. "There's always that pressure. There's that pressure with all the characters. When you're dealing with, as I have
for many, many years, with characters that are this loved and
this respected," Feige explained. But he had come a long way
from when he started with *X-Men* and people used to say, in
Feige's words, "Oh, 'X-Men'—you know it's going to suck because it's a *Marvel* movie."[8]

What's even more astounding than the original success of
Marvel's movies in Phase One was their success in Phase Two.
It's incredibly difficult to create good sequels and keep film
franchises going.[9] In the face of that, Feige and his team
brought movies to the screen that were fan favorites and
brought in billions of dollars. How would he do it again?

On Feige's nine-film slate were three individual superhero
sequels, a semi-sequel with an existing hero that also intro-

duced a new superhero to that storyline, three films introducing new superheroes, and two Avengers sequels which would bring the current ensemble's story cycle to an end.

The sequels Marvel launched in Phase Three were *Captain America: Civil War*, *Guardians of the Galaxy 2*, *Thor: Ragnarock*, and *Ant-Man and the Wasp*. Though they were continuations of their individual heroes' stories, these sequels also explored new territory. "It's easy for us as a group to come up with conceptually what we want to do," said Joe Russo, co-director with his brother Anthony of *Captain America: The Winter Soldier*, who agreed to direct *Civil War*, "and then we will ask questions about whether this would interfere with a storyline in another movie. Or, what's going on in that film, can we pull some of that into this film? That's where you start looking for the interconnectedness, but it's very important early on that the concept be created in a bubble because you have to protect the idea, it has to be driven by storytelling. Kevin's very good about just attacking each movie as they come and then figuring out what the movies are after that. Because if you get ahead of yourself two things can happen. One is you take your eye off the ball and you make a mess of a movie, and then the second thing that would happen is then you don't get to make any more movies. So he's always in the mindset of 'let's just make this movie now and worry about the next movie when it comes.'"[10]

Civil War not only introduced Spider-Man back into the Marvel Cinematic Universe, it showed greater depth in the character of Captain American and it pitted the two biggest heroes— Captain American and Iron Man—against each other in what seemed like an unresolvable conflict.

In *Thor: Ragnarock*, Feige sought out a director to change things up again: Taika Waititi. "It was really *Boy* that convinced us. And it was the meetings with Taika," said Feige of the choice to hire Waititi as director. The native of New Zealand got his start doing comedic short films that often relied on improvisation. He brought a different take on Thor that Feige loved. "He always knew he wanted to do a movie like this," said Feige. "He always knew he had a bigger scale movie in him. And I think he trusted that we wanted to do different things with the characters. He had done a sizzle reel that he had brought to our first meeting, that was hilarious—just clips from other movies, clips from other Thor movies, cut together with his own unique take and tone. And he used [Led Zeppelin's] 'Immigrant Song' in that sizzle reel. And it just unlocked a whole new thing for us. We went: 'This is it, this has got to be in the movie, this song's got to be in the marketing.' And, of course, it was."[11]

For *Guardians of the Galaxy Vol. 2,* James Gunn returned as director. In this sequel, Peter Quill explores his heritage, discovering and meeting the father he had never known. Gunn wanted a Marvel character named Ego to be Quill's father in the story. The only problem was that Ego was originally related to the Fantastic Four, which was controlled by Twentieth Century Fox. (Remember all the unfavorable deals Marvel used to make?) But Marvel and Gunn were in luck. The people at Fox making *Deadpool* wanted to change the abilities of one of Marvel's characters whose rights it had: Negasonic Teenage Warhead, a mutant with psychic powers. However, the contract Fox had agreed to stipulated that any changes to a character required Marvel's permission. So Marvel and Fox made a trade.[12] Marvel got to use Ego, and Fox was able to give Negasonic Teenage Warhead the ability to create explosions. And a precedent of cooperation between two competing studios was set, opening the door to other future possibilities.

In *Ant-Man and the Wasp*, Marvel introduced the Wasp as a new superhero, showing not only her origin story, but revealing information about her parents, who were the original Ant-Man and Wasp. It was also the first Marvel movie to feature a female hero in the title. Peyton Reed, who directed the original *Ant-Man*, returned to direct this sequel. And Paul Rudd, who played Ant-Man, collaborated with the movie's writers, as he did in the first movie. The sequel was successful, making over $100 million more than the original. In fact, every one of those sequels made more money at the box office than the movie that preceded it.

Groundbreaking New Superheroes

The most innovate work Feige and his team did during Phase Three involved three new characters who broke new ground and went on to take prominent places in the completion of the Avengers' story. Just as *Guardians of the Galaxy, Vol. 2* and *Thor: Ragnarock* made it possible for filmmakers to, as Feige expressed it, "explore the other aspects" of the Marvel Cinematic Universe,[13] *Doctor Strange* gave Marvel Studios the opportunity to add magic and the mystic arts to the world Marvel had created on screen.

"Doctor Strange, the Master of the Mystic Arts, Sorcerer Supreme—the whole notion of sorcerers, the whole notion of the multiverse and these parallel dimensions, is really important in the comic storylines," said Feige, "and we wanted to have access to that in our stories. Doctor Strange was always the in-point. It was in the visual effects reviews, in post-production, after we had shot most of the movie, that we really realized the mind-bending was going to work."[14]

By the time Marvel was looking for the right person to direct *Doctor Strange*, not only were professionals in the industry interested—they were competing to get on board the Marvel train. One of the candidates Feige and his team were considering was Scott Derrickson, who *really* wanted the job.

❝ Doctor Strange, the Master of the Mystic Arts, Sorcerer Supreme—the whole notion of sorcerers, the whole notion of the multiverse and these parallel dimensions, is really important in the comic storylines."

"I spent an extreme amount of money in creating my visual presentation to get this job," said Derrickson. "I spent an obnoxious amount of my own money. I did storyboards—I hired professional storyboard artists. I pre-wrote a twelve-page scene in the movie and illustrated it completely and created my own concept art. [Then] I went in and did a 90-minute presentation that cost me a LOT of money."

"He was inspired by the comics, turned it into a pitch. The two [elements] that I remember off the top of my head was the window doorways in the Sanctum leading to like a desert and an ocean and a forest. And what became the Astral Battle scene in the O.R., Strange's body's on the table, which he adapted out of a little bit out of *The Oath*,"[15] said Feige, describing the scene where Strange's spirit fought against an enemy's while Christine, played by Rachel McAdams, works on his chest wound.

"I was committed," said Derrickson. "I was going to out-spend every competing director. . . . I just knew that to get the job I had to show that I wanted it more than anyone."[16]

Derrickson's casting lived up to the Marvel standard, with respected actor Benedict Cumberbatch, described by one writer as an "art-house favorite" [17] in the title role, and Tilda Swinton in a role originally depicted in the comic books as an old man. The film not only introduced the multiverse into the Marvel Cinematic Universe, it also turned a relatively minor and obscure comic book character into another major on-screen force, told a fantastic story, and at $677 million, earned more than four times its budget.

While the introduction of the multiverse broke new ground for storytelling in future Marvel movies, *Black Panther* and *Captain Marvel* broke ground in other ways. While Black Panther may not have been the first black Marvel superhero to appear on screen—remember, Wesley Snipes played Blade in three movies—he certainly made the greatest impact. It was a big blockbuster superhero film dominated by African Americans—director Ryan Coogler, an avid comic book fan who was not only the first African American but also the youngest person to direct a Marvel film; a co-writer (with Coogler) Joe Robert Cole; plus a bunch of key production staff members that included executive producer Nate Moore, production director Hannah Beachler, costume designer Ruth E. Carter, hair department head Camille Friend, and specialty jeweler Douriean Fletcher.[18]

First and most importantly, *Black Panther* was a well-told story, which is always Marvel's first objective. Audiences loved it—the film received a rating of 96 percent on Rotten Tomatoes[19]—and for good reason. It depicted an idealized society in the African nation of Wakanda, led by a noble king T'Challa, played by Chadwick Boseman. It contained multitudes of strong female characters. It dealt with serious issues, showing characters reacting to racial and social injustice in three different ways:

isolation, revolution, and compassion. And it did all this with humor and pathos, while earning $1.3 billion at the box office.

"What Ryan Coogler ended up doing," said Feige, "and the way the audience responded, and then the acclaim and the box office numbers behind it, exceeded even our wildest expectations. And it's a tribute to Coogler, who is a brilliant, brilliant filmmaker and a humble, humble man. He tapped into very real questions that he had growing up, and still has growing up today, and he answered them in a cinematic way that I think ranks as one of the best ways that a filmmaker has ever expressed himself or his questions or his views on life in a feature. It was astounding to watch and astounding to see him put it together. And the response to it! I would say we've been surprised at Marvel Studios two or three times—none more so than [by] the amazing response, and the continued response, to *Black Panther*."[20] That response also included a nomination for best picture by the Academy of Motion Pictures. Though it didn't win in that category, it did win Oscars for costuming, production design, and score.[21]

We've been surprised at Marvel Studios two or three times—none more so than [by] the amazing response, and the continued response, to *Black Panther*."

Captain Marvel was the studio's first feature film whose main character was a female superhero. In front of the camera was Academy Award-winning actress Brie Larson. Behind it was a host of women, starting with Marvel's first female director,

Anna Boden, who also co-wrote the screenplay; writers Geneva Robertson-Dworet, Nicole Perlman, and Meg LeFauve; executive producers Victoria Alonso and Patricia Whitcher; plus a female composer, costume designer, and a host of art directors.[22]

At the time *Captain Marvel* was being filmed, Feige was asked about the role of women in Marvel's movies. "From the beginning of my career, the notion of the damsel in distress was outdated," said Feige, echoing the words of Stan Lee in 1961 when he stated that he wanted Susan Storm to be a superhero and active member of the Fantastic Four. "And when we started to make our own movies, we didn't want to fall into that trope—we wanted to avoid it as much as possible. With Agent Carter [in *Captain America*], she is unbelievably capable at a time when it was very difficult to rise up the ranks in the military. We really wanted to create these female characters that were as strong and as capable as the heroes.

"Now, as we've continued to grow, that's gotten even more apparent, to the point where they are the heroes. Literally right this second, Brie Larson is on the set of *Captain Marvel* in the first few weeks of photography; Evangeline Lilly has finished her role as the Wasp in *Ant-Man and the Wasp*—and it will only grow from there. What Ryan Coogler did with Okoye, Nakia, and Shuri in *Black Panther* . . . they're already iconic characters, and people are already asking, 'When are they getting their movies? When are we getting the Shuri movie?' The answer is: Nobody wants to see that more than me. And that's a testament to that film and to those actresses. And to the world being ready, and overdue, to see these types of characters on the screen."[23]

Audiences loved Captain Marvel's origin story and the strength of the character. *Glamour* magazine called her "a new kind of female hero," saying of the woman who becomes Captain

Marvel, "Carol Danvers is an Earth-born fighter pilot in the U.S. military. She's one of us, she's achievable. She shares our stories, our struggles in the real world . . . and unlike Wonder Woman, her super-suit neither hugs her hips nor exposes her skin." *Captain Marvel* earned more than $1 billion at the box office.[24] And the superhero became a vital character in the Avengers story.

> ❝❝ Nobody wants to see [Okoye, Nakia, and Shuri in movies] more than me. And that's a testament to that film and to those actresses. And to the world being ready, and overdue, to see these types of characters on the screen."

The End of the Avengers?

The resounding culmination planned for Phase Three consisted of two final Avengers movies: *Infinity War* and *Endgame*, both directed by Joe and Anthony Russo. They provided continuity which was a challenge since *all* of the superheroes from Marvel's other 19 films—plus Spider-Man—were to take part in the action. The villain of those movies, Thanos can be traced back though Marvel's other movies. "Thanos goes back with us to the very end of Phase One," said Feige, "to those last shots of Thanos at the end of the very first Avengers film. Joss wrote him into the script—he just turns around, you see his little smirk.

And that really was the beginning of us beginning to seed his grand story arc."[25] Thanos also appeared during Phase Two in *Guardians of the Galaxy*, as did an Infinity Stone. Both become important in the last two Avengers movies.

"It really was sort of *Iron Man 2* and building the architecture of the entire Phase One, that [the Infinity Stones] started to come about," said Feige, "and the notion of the Tesseract being not only the thing that ties Phase One together, but that also can be a part of all the things that tie Phase Two together. So I wouldn't say it was all perfectly planned and laid out in 2009, but that was the genesis of it. It goes back that far."[26]

Feige continued, "Well, some of it comes from the source material. The Cosmic Cube was always really important for Red Skull and for Captain America. We always knew in this film, *Age of Ultron*, that there was one [Infinity Stone] in Loki's scepter, and that was going to end up in Vision's forehead. And some of the other [Infinity Stones] . . . come out of a structural plot need sometimes for a McGuffin." (The term *McGuffin* is used in films to describe an object that has to be obtained, such as the Ark of the Covenant in *Raiders of the Lost Ark* or the bird statue in *The Maltese Falcon*.) "And the filmmaker will say, 'Okay, there's this orb in this,' and 'We'll go, okay, let's put something inside that orb and have it tie in to the larger mythology.'"[27]

Though the two films debuted almost exactly a year apart, as far as production was concerned, they were treated as one enormous project. Screenwriters Christopher Markus and Stephen McFeely, who had worked on all three Captain America films, as well as *Thor: The Dark World*, were hired to write both scripts and began working in late 2015. Pre-production started for both films in the spring of 2016, with principle photography beginning in January of 2017. In post-production, *Infinity War* received more than 2,900 visual effects,[28] while *Endgame* used more than 3,000.[29]

In all that, it could have been easy for everyone to lose sight of what they were trying to accomplish. But Robert Downey Jr., always the ringleader, helped the actors on set. Chadwick Boseman said of Downey, "He really does keep it so we're not focusing on the machine, that we are focusing on the humanity."[30]

Josh Brolin, who played Thanos, described the experience on set. "It's the right collective," he said. "It's like, back when you used to have all these theater collectives, and they're all working together putting this thing on and trying to find the color in everything, and the social significance, and all this stuff. And that's what makes Marvel films stand out: the feeling that somebody gave a theater troupe 500 million dollars by accident and they're all kind of adolescently, in the most beautiful sense of the word, so into what might happen. They're like, 'How can we paint ourselves into a corner,' and then, 'how will we find our way out?' Like, 'wouldn't it be cool if that guy just suddenly did this,' and it all comes together!"[31]

Before *Endgame* was released, Feige said it will bring "things you've never seen in superhero films: a finale. There will be two distinct periods. Everything before *[Endgame]* and everything after. I know it will not be in ways people are expecting."[32]

The final Avengers movies broke records. *Infinity War*, which debuted in April 2018, earned more than $2 billion worldwide, and *Endgame*, which was released in April of 2019, earned nearly $2.8 billion. All told, all 21 Marvel Studios movies (not including the Spider-Man movies they produced for Sony) earned an incredible $18.2 billion.[33] That made it the most lucrative franchise in movies history—bringing in almost double the next highest earner, *Star Wars*, and far exceeding the other top-grossing franchises: *Harry Potter, James Bond*, and *The Lord of the Rings*.[34]

> " That's what makes Marvel films stand out: the feeling that somebody gave a theater troupe 500 million dollars by accident and they're all kind of adolescently, in the most beautiful sense of the word, so into what might happen. They're like, 'How can we paint ourselves into a corner,' and then, 'how will we find our way out?' Like, 'wouldn't it be cool if that guy just suddenly did this,' and it all comes together!"

Joe Russo said, "We've been doing this for a long time and worked with just about everybody in the business. Kevin is just truly one of the most interesting people I've ever worked with in the business, probably one of the only people I've ever come across who could have pulled off a movie like *The Avengers*. He knew how difficult it is to line up those kinds of salaries and stars, get that material pushed through, have ownership of that material, have control of the material—quality control—to the extent that he did. It's almost impossible."[35]

Phase Four and More

While Feige and his team were bringing Phase Three to a close and doing the preliminary work for Phase Four, Disney made a move that benefited Marvel Studios. Disney chairman Bob Iger decided to buy Fox. He was motivated by the changing landscape of content delivery through streaming. With plans to launch Disney+, a streaming service to compete with Netflix, Amazon Prime Video, and others, he wanted Disney to have additional content to deliver through his service. Iger said, "Combining Disney's and 21st Century Fox's wealth of creative content and proven talent creates the preeminent global entertainment company, well positioned to lead in an incredibly dynamic and transformative era."[36]

While Disney planned to create shows for Disney+, including *The Falcon and the Winter Soldier*, *WandaVision*, *Loki*, *Hawkeye*, and *She-Hulk*, Marvel Studios got back the rights to the characters that had been licensed to Fox. When the deal was announced in late 2017, a Disney press release said, "The agreement also provides Disney with the opportunity to reunite the X-Men, Fantastic Four and Deadpool with the Marvel family under one roof and create richer, more complex worlds of inter-related characters and stories that audiences have shown they love."[37]

"Well, it's simple," Feige said. "When it all comes together, Marvel will have access to almost all of its characters, and that's something that most companies that have intellectual property characters have always had. . . . That just seems like something that's very appropriate and exciting for me—at the potential and the possibilities to come."[38]

On March 20, 2019, less than a month before *Endgame* debuted in theaters, Disney purchased Fox for $71.3 billion.[39] Marvel finally had all of their characters back except Spider-Man, and after *Spider-Man: Far from Home* came out, the cooperative agreement between Marvel and Sony ended.[40] Could Marvel buy Sony to get him back? Possibly. But what could be more likely is that Sony might be purchased by another studio or a company like Apple looking for content in its library. The way Sony's license is written, if it gets sold, the rights to Spider-Man would revert to Marvel.[41] So Marvel may end up with its entire catalog in the end.

At the time of this writing, Kevin Feige and his team are planning out the next five years of movies in the Marvel Cinematic Universe. They are writing screenplays and casting actors. The announced offerings, which include more women and greater diversity, include *Black Widow, Eternals, Shang-Chi and the Legend of the Ten Rings, Doctor Strange in the Multiverse of Madness, Thor: Love and Thunder, Black Panther II*, a reboot of *Blade, Guardians of the Galaxy Vol. 3, Captain Marvel 2*, and *Deadpool 3*, plus new movies featuring the Fantastic Four and X-Men.[42]

"I've always believed in expanding the definition of what a Marvel Studios movie could be. We try to keep audiences coming back in greater numbers by doing the unexpected and not simply following a pattern or a mold or a formula," said Feige.[43] Marvel is "Twenty-two movies in, and we've got another twenty movies on the docket that are completely different from anything that's come before—intentionally."[44]

It's difficult to say what's ahead for Marvel Studios. Certainly more creativity. If Feige and his team keep pushing the envelope in their selection of directors, if they keep up their record of extraordinary casting, if they keep exploiting all the innovations offered by the great leaps in visual effects, and if they keep getting the business support from parent company Disney—in other words, if they just keep doing what they're doing—there's almost no limit to what they could accomplish. After all, they have one of the deepest and riches wells of intellectual property created over eighty years by Martin Goodman, Stan Lee, Jack Kirby, Steve Ditko, and countless others. As Feige says, "In big ways and small ways, of course, this all starts from the House of Ideas in New York."[45]

❝ I've always believed in expanding the definition of what a Marvel Studios movie could be. We try to keep audiences coming back in greater numbers by doing the unexpected and not simply following a pattern or a mold or a formula . . . and we've got another twenty movies on the docket that are completely different from anything that's come before—intentionally."

ENDNOTES

Introduction

1. Arthur Meier Schlesinger, *The Rise of the City: 1878-1898* (New York: Macmillan, 1933), 185.
2. John Locke, "The Rise and Fall of Pulps," The Pulp Magazines Project, accessed June 21, 2019, https://www.pulpmags.org /contexts/graphs/rise-and-fall-of-pulps.html.
3. Louis Menand, "Pulp's Big Moment," New Yorker, December 29, 2014, https://www.newyorker.com/magazine/2015/01/05 /pulps-big-moment.
4. Les Daniels, *Marvel: Five Fabulous Decades of the World's Greatest Comics* (New York: Abrams, 1993), 17.
5. Blake Bell and Michael J. Vassallo, *The Secret History of Marvel Comics* (Seattle: Fantagraphics Books, 2013), 12.
6. David Saunders, "Louis H. Silberkleit," Field Guide to Wild American Pulp Artists, posted in 2016, https://www.pulpartists .com/Goodman.html.
7. David Saunders, "Martin Goodman," Field Guide to Wild American Pulp Artists, posted in 2016, https://www.pulpartists.com /Goodman.html.
8. Blake Bell and Michael J. Vassallo, *The Secret History*, 7.
9. David Saunders, "Martin Goodman."
10. Blake Bell and Michael J. Vassallo, *The Secret History*, 45.
11. Blake Bell and Michael J. Vassallo, 22.
12. Les Daniels, *Marvel: Five Fabulous Decades*, 16.
13. Brian Truitt, "Copy of 'Action Comics' No. 1 Sells for $3.21 Million," *USA Today*, August 24, 2014, https://www.usatoday.com /story/life/2014/08/24/action-comics-no-1-most-expensive -comic-book/14545215.

14. Les Daniels, *Marvel: Five Fabulous Decades*, 23.

15. Adam Pockross, "10 Most Valuable Marvel Comic Books," Screen Rant, November, 5, 2015, https://screenrant.com/most-valuable-marvel-superhero-comic-books/.

16. Bob Batchelor, *Stan Lee: The Man Behind Marvel* (Lanham, MD: Roman and Littlefield, 2017), 23.

17. Kevin Melrose, "Marvel's Character Library: 7,000 Strong . . . and Growing?" CBR.com, March 4, 2010, https://www.cbr.com/marvels-character-library-7000-strong-and-growing.

18. "Characters," Marvel Database, accessed July 9, 2019, https://marvel.fandom.com/wiki/Category:Characters.

19. "Characters," DC Database, accessed July 9, 2019, https://dc.fandom.com/wiki/Category:Characters.

20. Matt Patches, "History: Batman and Superman—Partners, Fighters, Bed Sharers," Vulture, July 26, 2013, https://www.vulture.com/2013/07/history-batman-and-superman-through-the-years.html.

21. Mark Alexander, *Lee and Kirby: The Wonder Years* (Raleigh, NC: Two Morrows, 2011), 11.

22. Bob Batchelor, *Stan Lee*, 24.

23. Les Daniels, *Marvel: Five Fabulous Decades*, 37.

24. Richard Harrington, "Stan Lee: Caught in Spidey's Web," the *Washington Post*, February 4, 1992, https://www.washingtonpost.com/archive/lifestyle/1992/02/04/stan-lee-caught-in-spideys-web/9e7bf42e-4287-4f9c-9fa1-a5f73fb2ee7e/?utm_term=.91f7df980142.

25. Anthony Breznican, "The Face of Marvel," *Stan Lee: A Life of Marvel* (New York: Time Inc. Books, 2018), 52.

26. Blake Bell and Michael J. Vassallo, *The Secret History*, 101.

27. Stan Lee and George Mair, *Excelsior*, (New York: Simon & Schuster, 2002), 25.

28. Richard Harrington, "Stan Lee."

29. Blake Bell and Michael J. Vassallo, *The Secret History*, 23.

30. Les Daniels, *Marvel: Five Fabulous Decades*, 40.

31. Les Daniels, 49.

32. "Where was I going?" Richard Harrington, "Stan Lee."

33. Blake Bell and Michael J. Vassallo, *The Secret History*, 91–92.

34. Blake Bell and Michael J. Vassallo, 92.

35. Alex Pappademas, "The Inquisition of Mr. Marvel," Grantland, May 11, 2012, http://grantland.com/features/the-surprisingly -complicated-legacy-marvel-comics-legend-stan-lee.

36. Bob Batchelor, *Stan Lee*, 59.

37. Les Daniels, *Marvel: Five Fabulous Decades*, 80.

38. Richard Harrington, "Stan Lee."

Chapter 1

1. Cefn Ridout (ed.), *Marvel Year by Year: A Visual History* (New York: DK, 2017), 78.

2. Stan Lee and George Mair, *Excelsior*, 111–112.

3. Les Daniels, *Marvel: Five Fabulous Decades*, 81.

4. Stan Lee and George Mair, *Excelsior*, 113.

5. Richard Harrington, "Stan Lee."

6. Richard Harrington.

7. Richard Harrington.

8. Richard Harrington.

9. Stan Lee, "A History of Comics," 39.

10. Richard Harrington, "Stan Lee."

11. Stan Lee, "A History of Comics," 39.

12. Anthony Breznican, "The Face of Marvel," 54.

13. Richard Harrington, "Stan Lee."

14. Anthony Breznican, "The Face of Marvel," 55.

15. IMDb Pro, compiled box office figures for *Spider-Man, Spider-Man 2, Spider-Man 3, The Amazing Spider-Man, The Amazing Spider-Man 2, Spider-Man: Homecoming, Spider-Man: Far from Home*, and *Spider-Man: Into the Spiderverse*.

16. Cefn Ridout (ed.), *Marvel Year by Year*, 94.

17. Richard Harrington, "Stan Lee."

18. Richard Harrington.

19. Les Daniels, *Marvel: Five Fabulous Decades*, 158.

20. Stan Lee and George Mair, *Excelsior*, 179.

21. Sean Howe, *Marvel Comics: The Untold Story* (New York: Harper Perennial, 2012), 92.

22. Blake Bell and Michael J. Vassallo, *The Secret History*, 102.

23. Sean Howe, *Marvel Comics*, 122.

24. Stan Lee and George Mair, *Excelsior*, 183.

25. Stan Lee and George Mair, 182.
26. Les Daniels, *Marvel: Five Fabulous Decades*, 156.
27. Bob Batchelor, *Stan Lee*, 133.
28. Sean Howe, *Marvel Comics*, 323.
29. Sean Howe, 168.
30. Bob Chipman, "The Best (and Worst) Marvel Cartoons of the 60s and 70s," The Escapist, August 20, 2014, http://www.escapist magazine.com/articles/view/moviesandtv/columns/marveltv /12135-Marvel-Cartoons-of-the-60s-and-70s.
31. Sean Howe, *Marvel Comics*, 121.
32. Jordan Raphael and Tom Spurgeon, *Stan Lee*, 190.
33. Jordan Raphael and Tom Spurgeon, 190.
34. Jordan Raphael and Tom Spurgeon, 192–193.
35. Sean Howe, *Marvel Comics*, 195–196.
36. Jordan Raphael and Tom Spurgeon, *Stan Lee*, 191.
37. Jordan Raphael and Tom Spurgeon, 191.
38. Bob Batchelor, *Stan Lee*, 156.
39. Jordan Raphael and Tom Spurgeon, *Stan Lee*, 185.
40. Bob Batchelor, *Stan Lee*, 154.
41. Sean Howe, *Marvel Comics*, 261.
42. Sean Howe, 263.
43. Sean Howe, 264.
44. "Marvel Entertainment Group, Inc. History," Funding Universe, accessed July 25, 2019, http://www.fundinguniverse.com /company-histories/marvel-entertainment-group-inc-history/.
45. Sean Howe, *Marvel Comics*, 294.

Chapter 2

1. Sean Howe, *Marvel Comics*, 264.
2. Jonathan P. Hicks, "The Media Business; Marvel Comic Book Unit Being Sold for $82.5 Million," *New York Times*, November 8, 1988, https://www.nytimes.com/1988/11/08/business/the -media-business-marvel-comic-book-unit-being-sold-for-82.5 -million.html.
3. Sean Howe, *Marvel Comics*, 295.
4. Rob Kelly, "Reel Retro Cinema: 1944s Captain America Serial," 13th Dimension, accessed July 17, 2019, https://13thdimension .com/reel-retro-cinema-1944s-captain-america-serial/.

5. Sean Howe, *Marvel Comics*, 309–310.

6. "Fabulous Flop: How Howard the Duck Changed Hollywood," Portable Press (blog), August 5, 2013, https://www.portablepress .com/blog/2013/08/fabulous-flop-how-howard-the-duck -changed-hollywood.

7. "Howard the Duck (1986)," IMDb Pro, accessed July 26, 2019, https://pro.imdb.com/title/tt0091225?rf=cons_tt_atf&ref _=cons_tt_atf.

8. Sean Howe, *Marvel Comics*, 293.

9. "Howard the Duck (1986)," IMDb Pro.

10. Sean Howe, *Marvel Comics*, 309.

11. Jonathan P. Hicks, "The Media Business."

12. Al Delugach, "Jilting Paretti, New World Sells Out to Perelman for $145 Million," Los Angeles Times, April 11, 1989, https:// www.latimes.com/archives/la-xpm-1989-04-11-fi-1676-story.html.

13. Adam Bryant, "Pow! The Punches that Left Marvel Reeling," *New York Times*, May 24, 1998.

14. Sean Howe, *Marvel Comics*, 332.

15. Sean Howe, 343.

16. Sean Howe, 332.

17. Sean Howe, 339.

18. Fant v. Perelman, et al, 97cv08435, case number CV-97-TMP-1895-6, filed July 24, 1997, securities.stanford.edu, https://www.google .com/url?sa=t&rct=j&q=&esrc=s&source=web&cd=8&cad=rja &uact=8&ved=2ahUKEwjB_9LynqvkAhWqY98KHTOXCd QQFjAHegQIBBAB&url=http percent3A percent2F percent2F securities.stanford.edu percent2Ffilings-documents percent2 F1004 percent2FMRV97 percent2F001.html&usg=AOvVaw0xf BxTT-1EH3ZRUtKuYHIx.

19. "Marvel Entertainment Group, Inc. History."

20. Sean Howe, *Marvel Comics*, 350.

21. "Why Do the Avengers Fear this Man?" *The Telegraph*, April 29, 2015, https://www.telegraph.co.uk/culture/film/film-news /11560174/isaac-ike-perlmutter-marvel-owner.html.

22. Matthew Garrahan, "Man in the News: Ike Perlmutter, Financial Times, September 4, 2009, https://www.ft.com/content/4080 d0de-997f-11de-ab8c-00144feabdc0#axzz1wkuFZPBa.

23. April Dougal Gasbarre, "Toy Biz, Inc.," International Director of Company Histories, accessed July 29, 2019, https://www

.encyclopedia.com/books/politics-and-business-magazines
/toy-biz-inc.

24. Dan Raviv, *Comic Wars* (New York: Broadway Books, 2002), 41.

25. April Dougal Gasbarre, "Toy Biz, Inc."

26. Dan Raviv, *Comic Wars*, 39.

27. Dan Raviv, 39.

28. Dan Raviv, 40–41.

29. April Dougal Gasbarre, "Toy Biz, Inc."

30. Ryan Lambie, "How Marvel Went from Bankruptcy to Billions,"
    DenofGeek.com, April 17, 2018, https://www.denofgeek.com
    /us/books-comics/marvel/243710/how-marvel-went-from
    -bankruptcy-to-billions.

31. Sean Howe, *Marvel Comics*, 356.

32. Dan Raviv, *Comic Wars*, 8.

33. Geoff Boucher, "Avi Arad: From 'Blade' to 'Morbius,' Three
    Decades of Mining Marvel," Deadline, March 20, 2019, https://
    deadline.com/2019/03/avi-arad-marvel-blade-spider-man
    -morbius-toys-1202576569.

34. Dan Raviv, *Comic Wars*, 9.

35. Geoff Boucher, "Avi Arad."

36. Dan Raviv, *Comic Wars*, 41.

37. Sean Howe, *Marvel Comics*, 355.

38. Sean Howe, 355.

39. Ryan Lambie, "Bankruptcy to Billions."

40. Robert Ito, "Fantastic Faux," *Lost Angeles Magazine*, March 2005,
    106-111, 218-19, https://books.google.com/books?id=SF8EAA
    AAMBAJ&pg=PA109&dq= percent22selling+the+character
    percent27s+option+to+Universal percent22&hl=en&sa=X&ei
    =FJbjUPe3KMy70AHlwoDAAw&ved=0CD4Q6AEwAA#v=onepage
    &q= percent22selling percent20the percent20character's percent
    20option percent20to percent20Universal percent22&f=false.

41. "5 Spider-Man Movies that Almost Happened," Warped Factor,
    August 22, 2019, http://www.warpedfactor.com/2016/05/5
    -spider-man-movies-that-almost-happened.html.

42. Michael A. Hiltzik, "Studio Rights to Spider-Man Are Untan-
    gled," *Los Angeles Times*, March 2, 1999, https://www.latimes.com
    /archives/la-xpm-1999-mar-02-fi-13115-story.html.

43. Nancy Hass, "Investing It; Marvel Superheroes Take Aim at Hol-
    lywood, *New York Times*, July 28, 1996, https://www.nytimes.com

/1996/07/28/business/investing-it-marvel-superheroes-take
-aim-at-hollywood.html?searchResultPosition=1.

44. Sean Howe, *Marvel Comics*, 381.

45. Dan Raviv, *Comic Wars*, 49.

46. David Leonhart, "What Evil Lurks in the Heart of Ron?" *Business Week*, January 22, 1996, 44.

47. Sean Howe, *Marvel Comics*, 387.

48. Sean Howe, 386.

49. Sean Howe, 386–387.

50. Dan Raviv, *Comic Wars*, 243.

51. Sean Howe, *Marvel Comics*, 392.

52. Sean Howe, 392.

53. Sean Howe, 396.

Chapter 3

1. Sean Howe, *Marvel Comics*, 400.

2. Sean Howe, 398.

3. Fritz, Ben *The Big Picture: The Fight for the Future of Movies* (Boston: Houghton Mifflin Harcourt, 2018), 45.

4. Sean Howe, *Marvel Comics*, 399.

5. "Tomb of Dracula (1972) #10," Marvel.com, accessed September 4, 2019, https://www.marvel.com/comics/issue/11832/tomb_of_dracula_1972_10.

6. "Blade (1998)," IMDb Pro, accessed September 3, 2019, https://pro.imdb.com/title/tt0120611?rf=cons_tt_atf&ref_=cons_tt_atf.

7. Sean Howe, *Marvel Comics*, 396.

8. Geoff Boucher, "Avi Arad."

9. Ben Fritz, *The Big Picture*, 45–46.

10. Ben Fritz, 45–46.

11. "X-Men (2000)," IMDb Pro, accessed September 4, 2019, https://pro.imdb.com/title/tt0120903/details.

12. "X-Men (2000)."

13. "X-Men (2000)."

14. Joanna Robinson, "The Woman Behind the X-Men Reveals How the Mutants Got Their Groove Back," *Vanity Fair*, March 3, 2017, https://www.vanityfair.com/hollywood/2017/03/logan-legion-deadpool-x-men-renaissance-lauren-shuler-donner-interview.

15. Matthew Garrahan, "Kevin Feige: The Movie Nut," *Financial Times*, October 31, 2014.

16. "Kevin Feige—Cover Story," Producers Guild, December 13, 2016, https://www.producersguild.org/blogpost/1537650/264535/Kevin-Feige–Cover-Story.

17. "Kevin Feige—Cover Story."

18. "Kevin Feige—Cover Story."

19. "Kevin Feige—Cover Story."

20. Brooks Barnes, "With Fan at the Helm, Marvel Safely Steers Its Heroes to the Screen," *New York Times*, July 24, 2011, https://www.nytimes.com/2011/07/25/business/media/marvel-with-a-fan-at-the-helm-steers-its-heroes-to-the-screen.html?pagewanted=all.

21. Kelly Konda, "How the MCU Was Made: Lauren Shuler Donner Lets Kevin Feige Sit In," We Minored in Film, April 23, 2019, https://weminoredinfilm.com/2019/04/23/how-the-mcu-was-made-lauren-shuler-donner-lets-kevin-feige-sit-in.

22. Kervyn Cloete, "The Marvel Cinematic Universe Exists Because of Hugh Jackman's Hair," Critical Hit Entertainment, posted November 30, 2017, https://www.criticalhit.net/entertainment/marvel-cinematic-universe-exists-hugh-jackmans-hair.

23. Kervyn Cloete.

24. "X-Men (2000)," IMDb Pro.

25. "X-Men (2000)."

26. Dan Raviv, *Comic Wars*, 272.

27. Ben Fritz, *The Big Picture*, 50.

28. Sean Howe, *Marvel Comics*, 405.

29. Sean Howe, 403.

30. Sean Howe, 401.

31. Geoff Boucher, "Avi Arad."

32. Sean Howe, *Marvel Comics*, 397.

33. "Spider-Man (2002)," IMDb Pro, accessed September 5, 2019, https://pro.imdb.com/title/tt0145487/details.

34. "Spider-Man (2002)."

35. "Spider-Man (2002)."

36. Sean Howe, *Marvel Comics*, 415.

37. Ben Fritz, *The Big Picture*, 50.

38. Ben Fritz, 50.

39. Ben Fritz, 50.

40. Sean Howe, *Marvel Comics*, 417.

41. Ben Fritz, *The Big Picture*, 50.

42. Ben Fritz, 53.

43. Ben Fritz, 50.

44. Ben Fritz, 51.

45. Ben Fritz, 51.

46. Sean Howe, *Marvel Comics*, 417.

47. Ben Fritz, *The Big Picture*, 49.

48. Devin Leonard, "Calling All Superheroes," *Fortune*, May 23, 2007, https://archive.fortune.com/magazines/fortune/fortune _archive/2007/05/28/100034246/index.htm.

49. "Box Office History for Spider-Man Movies," The Numbers, accessed September 6, 2019, https://m.the-numbers.com/movies /franchise/Spider-Man.

50. Ben Fritz, *The Big Picture*, 49.

51. James Whitbrook, "The Complete History of Marvel Superhero Movies: 1990-2008, io9, March 17, 2015, https://io9.gizmodo. com/the-complete-history-of-marvel-superhero-movies-1990-2 -1691891718.

52. Devin Leonard, "Calling All Superheroes."

53. Dan Raviv, *Comic Wars*, 270–271.

54. Sean Howe, *Marvel Comics*, 417.

55. Sean Howe, 398.

56. Alex Pappademas, "The Inquisition of Mr. Marvel."

57. Sean Howe, *Marvel Comics*, 426.

58. Alex Pappademas, "The Inquisition of Mr. Marvel."

59. Ben Fritz, *The Big Picture*, 54.

60. Ben Fritz, 55.

61. Ben Fritz, 55.

62. Kim Masters, "Marvel Studios' Origin Secrets Revealed by Mysterious Founder: History was Rewritten," *Hollywood Reporter*, May 5, 2016, https://www.hollywoodreporter.com/features/marvel -studios-origin-secrets-revealed-889795.

63. Kim Masters.

64. Ben Fritz, *The Big Picture*, 56.

65. Ben Fritz, 56.

66. Kim Masters, "Origin Secrets Revealed."

67. Kim Masters.

68. Kim Masters.

69. Ben Fritz, *The Big Picture*, 56.

70. Ben Fritz, 57.

71. Ben Fritz, 56.

72. Kim Masters, "Origin Secrets Revealed."

73. Kim Masters.

74. Ben Fritz, *The Big Picture*, 57.

75. Kim Masters, "Origin Secrets Revealed."

76. Kim Masters.

77. Kim Masters.

78. Ben Fritz, *The Big Picture*, 58.

79. Kim Masters, "Origin Secrets Revealed."

80. Ben Fritz, *The Big Picture*, 59.

81. "Iron Man (2008)," IMDb Pro, accessed May 30, 2019, https://pro.imdb.com/title/tt0371746/details.

82. Kim Masters, "Origin Secrets Revealed."

83. Sean Howe, "Avengers Assemble! How Marvel Went from Hollywood Also-ran to Mastermind of a $1 Billion Franchise," Slate, September 28, 2012, https://slate.com/business/2012/09/marvel-comics-and-the-movies-the-business-story-behind-the-avengers.html.

84. Ben Fritz, *The Big Picture*, 60.

85. Ben Fritz, 59.

86. Ben Fritz, 59.

87. Ben Fritz, 61.

88. Ben Fritz, 61.

89. Ben Fritz, 57.

90. Sean Howe, *Marvel Comics*, 426.

91. Kim Masters, "Origin Secrets Revealed."

92. Joanna Robinson, "Marvel Looks Back at Iron Man—the Movie That Started It All," *Vanity Fair*, November 29, 2017, https://www.vanityfair.com/hollywood/2017/11/marvel-looks-back-at-iron-man-the-movie-that-started-it-all.

93. Kim Masters, "Origin Secrets Revealed."

Chapter 4

1. Joel Meares, "Kevin Feige's Oral History of the Marvel Cinematic Universe," Rotten Tomatoes, April 23, 2018, https://editorial .rottentomatoes.com/article/kevin-feiges-oral-history-of-the -marvel-cinematic-universe.
2. Sean Howe, *Marvel Comics*, 427.
3. "Avi Arad Leaving Marvel to Be Independent Producer," ICV2, posted May 31, 2006, https://icv2.com/articles/comics/view /8770/avi-arad-leaving-marvel.
4. Ben Fritz, *The Big Picture*, 65.
5. Ben Fritz, 63.
6. Sean Howe, *Marvel Comics*, 427.
7. Joanna Robinson, "Marvel Looks Back."
8. Ben Fritz, *The Big Picture*, 62.
9. Ben Fritz, 62.
10. Kim Masters, "Origin Secrets Revealed."
11. Ben Fritz, *The Big Picture*, 63.
12. Ben Fritz, 63.
13. "Iron Man (2008)," IMDb Pro.
14. "Iron Man (2008)."
15. "Iron Man (2008)."
16. "Iron Man (2008)."
17. "Iron Man (2008)."
18. "Iron Man (2008)."
19. Ben Fritz, *The Big Picture*, 62.
20. Joanna Robinson, "Marvel Looks Back."
21. Ben Fritz, *The Big Picture*, 63.
22. "Iron Man (2008)," IMDb Pro.
23. "Jon Favreau," IMDb Pro, accessed September 10, 2019, https:// pro.imdb.com/name/nm0269463?rf=cons_nm_contact&ref _=cons_nm_contact.
24. Ben Fritz, *The Big Picture*, 64.
25. "Iron Man Production Notes," from original Paramount Pictures's Iron Man website (ironmanmovie.com), reposted by Sci-FiJapan, April 30, 2008, http://www.scifijapan.com/articles /2008/04/30/iron-man-production-notes.
26. Joanna Robinson, "Marvel Looks Back."
27. "Iron Man Production Notes."

28. "Iron Man (2008)," IMDb Pro.

29. Joanna Robinson, "Marvel Looks Back."

30. Edward Douglas, "Exclusive: An In-Depth Iron Man Talk with Jon Favreau," SuperHeroHype!, April 29, 2008, https://www.superherohype.com/features/96427-exclusive-an-in-depth-iron-man-talk-with-jon-favreau.

31. Edward Douglas, "Talk with Jon Favreau."

32. "Kevin Feige—Cover Story," Producers Guild.

33. "Iron Man Production Notes."

34. "Iron Man Production Notes."

35. Joel Meares, "Kevin Feige's Oral History."

36. "Iron Man (2008)," IMDb Pro.

37. Edward Douglas, "Talk with Jon Favreau."

38. "Iron Man Production Notes."

39. "Iron Man Production Notes."

40. "Iron Man Production Notes."

41. Devin Faraci, "The Marvel Creative Committee is Over," Birth.Movies.Death, September 2, 2015, https://birthmoviesdeath.com/2015/09/02/the-marvel-creative-committee-is-over.

42. Ben Fritz, *The Big Picture*, 65.

43. Sean Howe, *Marvel Comics*, 427.

44. Geoff Boucher, "Avi Arad."

45. Ben Fritz, *The Big Picture*, 64.

46. "Iron Man (2008)," IMDb Pro.

47. "Iron Man (2008)."

48. "Iron Man (2008)."

49. "Iron Man (2008)."

50. Edward Douglas, "Talk with Jon Favreau."

51. Ben Fritz, *The Big Picture*, 64–65.

52. Edward Douglas, "Talk with Jon Favreau."

53. "Iron Man Production Notes."

54. Scott Rabb, "May God Bless and Keep Robert Downey Jr." Esquire, February 21, 2007, https://www.esquire.com/news-politics/a2074/esq0307downeyjr.

55. Edward Douglas, "Talk with Jon Favreau."

56. Edward Douglas.

57. Joanna Robinson, "Marvel Looks Back."

58. Edward Douglas, "Exclusive: Marvel Studios Production Head Kevin Feige," Super Hero Hype, April 26, 2010, https://www.superherohype.com/features/100681-exclusive-marvel-studios-production-head-kevin-feige.

59. "Iron Man Production Notes."

60. Scott Rabb, "God Bless Robert Downey Jr."

61. "Iron Man (2008)," IMDb Pro.

62. "Iron Man Production Notes."

63. Edward Douglas, "Talk with Jon Favreau."

64. "Iron Man (2008)," IMDb Pro.

65. "Iron Man (2008)."

66. "Iron Man Production Notes."

67. Edward Douglas, "Talk with Jon Favreau."

68. Kim Masters, "Origin Secrets Revealed."

69. Ben Fritz, *The Big Picture*, 68.

70. Ashley Rodriguez, "Iron Man Went from a B-hero to Marvel's Movie Star Because He had the Best Toys," Quartz, May 3, 1018, https://qz.com/1267000/iron-man-launched-the-marvel-cinematic-universe-because-he-had-the-best-toys.

71. Ben Fritz, *The Big Picture*, 68.

72. Ben Fritz, 68.

73. Joanna Robinson, "Marvel Looks Back."

74. Joanna Robinson.

75. Ashley Rodriguez, "From B-hero to Marvel's Star."

76. Ashley Rodriguez.

77. Joanna Robinson, "Marvel Looks Back."

78. Ben Fritz, *The Big Picture*, 69.

79. "Jon Favreau," IMDb Pro.

80. Joanna Robinson, "Marvel Looks Back."

81. Ben Fritz, *The Big Picture*, 69.

82. Adam Chitwood, "How the MCU Was Made: 'The Incredible Hulk,'" Collider, April 22, 2019, http://collider.com/incredible-hulk-production-problems-explained/.

83. "Marvel Cinematic Universe Movies & TV Shows," Rotten Tomatoes, accessed September 12, 2019, https://www.rottentomatoes.com/franchise/marvel_cinematic_universe.

84. Ben Fritz, *The Big Picture*, 69.

Chapter 5

1. Stan Lee and George Mair, *Excelsior*, 183.

2. · Jim McLauchlin, "Disney's $4 Billion Marvel Buy."

3. Brooks Barnes and Michael Cieply, "Disney Swoops into Action, Buying Marvel for $4 Billion," *New York Times*, August 31, 2009, https://www.nytimes.com/2009/09/01/business/media/01 disney.html.

4. "Disney Completes Marvel Acquisition," The Walt Disney Company, December 31, 2009, https://www.thewaltdisneycompany .com/disney-completes-marvel-acquisition.

5. Pamela McClintock, "Move for Marvel Rights" *Variety*, October 18, 2010, https://www.webcitation.org/5zxBn7VD8?url=http:// www.variety.com/article/VR1118025864.html?categoryId =13&cs=1.

6. Marc Graser, "Why Par, not Disney, gets 'Avengers' credit," *Variety*, October 11, 2011, http://www.variety.com/article/VR1118044 282, archived from the original on October 12, 2011, https:// www.webcitation.org/62NajSZYC?url=http://www.variety .com/article/VR1118044282, Retrieved September 13, 2019.

7. Brooks Barnes and Michael Cieply, "Disney Swoops."

8. Brooks Barnes and Michael Cieply.

9. Matt Donnelly, "Meet the Executive Avengers Who Help Kevin Feige Make Marvel Magic," *Variety*, April 17, 2019, https://variety .com/2019/film/features/victoria-alonso-louis-desposito-marvel -studios-kevin-feige-avengers-1203189857.

10. Joanna Robinson, "Secrets of the Marvel Universe," *Vanity Fair*, November 27, 2017, https://www.vanityfair.com/hollywood /2017/11/marvel-cover-story.

11. Joanna Robinson.

12. Joanna Robinson.

13. Peter Sciretta, "Watch: All of Your Marvel Phase 3 Questions Answered by Marvel Head Kevin Feige," (interview transcript), /Film, October 28, 2014, https://www.slashfilm.com/marvel -phase-3-kevin-feige/.

14. Joel Meares, "Kevin Feige's Oral History."

15. Nicole LaPorte, "The Marvel Studios Mind-Set For Making Hit After Hit," Fast Company, March/April 2018, https://www

.fastcompany.com/40525480/the-marvel-studios-mind-set-for-making-hit-after-hit.

16. Scott Huver, "Feige & Latcham Say 'Infinity War' Leads to the End of the Avengers – As We Know Them," Comic Book Resources, September 30, 2015, https://www.cbr.com/feige-latcham-say-infinity-war-leads-to-the-end-of-the-avengers-as-we-know-them/.

17. "Kevin Feige on Upcoming Marvel Studios Films," Super Hero Hype, posted January 26, 2010, https://www.superherohype.com/features/100085-kevin-feige-on-upcoming-marvel-studios-films.

18. Chris Lee, "Thor: It's Hammer Time for Kenneth Branagh," *Newsweek*, May 1, 2011, https://www.newsweek.com/thor-its-hammer-time-kenneth-branagh-67665.

19. Ethan Alter, "How 'Thor' Opened Up the MCU: Kenneth Branagh on Hiring Chris Hemsworth, Going to Space, and the Terror of Fabio," Yahoo Finance, May 17, 2019, https://finance.yahoo.com/news/thor-chris-hemsworth-kenneth-branagh-tom-hiddleston-160246757.html.

20. Mark Graham, "Marvel Rolls Dice, Casts No-names for Thor," Vulture, May 19, 2009, https://www.vulture.com/2009/05/marvel_rolls_dice_casts_no-nam.html.

21. "Iron Man 2 (2010)," IMDb Pro, accessed September 17, 2019, https://pro.imdb.com/title/tt1228705/details.

22. "Thor (2011), IMDb Pro, accessed September 17, 2019, https://pro.imdb.com/title/tt0800369/details.

23. "Captain America: The First Avenger (2011)," IMDb Pro, accessed September 17, 2019, https://pro.imdb.com/title/tt0458339/?ref_=recent_view_7.

24. Jim Vejvoda, "Marvel Studios Boss Kevin Feige Talks Captain America: The Winder Soldier Spoilers and What's in Store for the Marvel Cinematic Universe," IGN, April 7, 2014, https://www.ign.com/articles/2014/04/07/marvel-studios-boss-kevin-feige-talks-captain-america-the-winter-soldier-spoilers-and-whats-in-store-for-the-marvel-cinematic-universe.

25. Edward Douglas, "Talk with Jon Favreau."

26. "Joss Whedon," IMDb Pro, accessed September 17, 2019, https://pro.imdb.com/name/nm0923736?rf=cons_nm_contact&ref_=cons_nm_contact.

27. Gus Lubin, "Joss Whedon Was Brutally Honest When He Saw The Original 'Avengers' Script," Business Insider, July 18, 2014, http://www.businessinsider.in/Joss-Whedon-Was-Brutally -Honest-When-He-Saw-The-Original-Avengers-Script/articleshow /38612600.cms.

28. Matt Patches and Ian Failes, "The Battle of New York: An 'Avengers' Oral History," Thrillist. April 23, 2018, https://www.thrillist .com/entertainment/nation/the-avengers-battle-of-new-york -joss-whedon.

29. Matt Patches and Ian Failes.

30. Joel Meares, "Kevin Feige's Oral History."

31. Mike Vilensky, "Mark Ruffalo on 'Actually' Playing the Hulk in The Avengers," New York, September 24, 2010, http://nymag.com /daily/entertainment/2010/09/mark_ruffalo_on_actually_playi .html.

32. Marvel Studios: The First Ten Years (London: Titan Publishing, 2018), 6.

33. Matt Donnelly, "How Gwyneth Paltrow was recruited for 'The Avengers,'" Los Angeles Times, April 17, 2012, http://www.latimes .com/entertainment/gossip/la-et-mg-gwyneth-paltrow-avengers, 0,311022.story. Archived from the original on June 23, 2012, retrieved September 13, 2019, https://www.webcitation.org /68duJTU9q?url=http://www.latimes.com/entertainment /gossip/la-et-mg-gwyneth-paltrow-avengers,0,311022.story.

34. Marvel Studios: The First Ten Years, 44.

35. "'The Avengers' Smashes Domestic Box Office Record for Opening Weekend," CNN, May 7, 2012, https://www.cnn.com /2012/05/06/showbiz/avengers-breaks-record/index.html.

36. Adam B. Vary, "Jon Favreau talks 'Iron Man,'" Entertainment Weekly, May 5, 2008, https://ew.com/article/2008/05/05/jon -favreau-talks-iron-man/.

37. Joel Meares, "Kevin Feige's Oral History."

38. Peter Travers, "The Avengers," Rolling Stone, April 30, 2012, https://www.rollingstone.com/movies/movie-reviews/the -avengers-118986/.

39. "The Avengers (2012)," IMDb Pro, accessed September 17, 2019, https://pro.imdb.com/title/tt0848228/?ref_=instant_tt _1&q=the percent20avengers.

40.   *Marvel Studios: The First Ten Years*, 4.

41.   Joel Meares, "Kevin Feige's Oral History."

42.   Peter Sciretta, "Your Marvel Phase 3 Questions."

43.   Eric Goldman, "The Winder Soldier: Has America Changed Too Much for Captain America?" IGN, posted March 6, 2014, https://www.ign.com/articles/2014/03/06/the-winter-soldier-has-america-changed-too-much-for-captain-america?page=4.

44.   Haleigh Foutch, "The Russo Brothers on What It Takes to Land a Marvel Directing Gig," Collider, April 30, 2016, http://collider.com/russo-brothers-captain-america-civil-war-interview/.

45.   Joel Meares, "Kevin Feige's Oral History."

46.   Joel Meares.

47.   *Marvel Studios: The First Ten Years*, 68.

48.   Eric Goldman, "The Winter Soldier."

49.   Nicole LaPorte, "The Marvel Studios Mind-Set"

50.   Adam B. Vary, "What's at Stake for Thor, Captain America, and The 'Avengers' Franchise," BuzzFeed News, October 28, 2014, https://www.buzzfeednews.com/article/adambvary/thor-captain-america-avengers-age-of-ultron-set-visit.

51.   Adam B. Vary.

52.   Adam B. Vary.

53.   Peter Sciretta, "Kevin Feige on How a Marvel Movie Like 'Doctor Strange' Is Developed, & Why Time Travel Won't Ruin the MCU," /film, November 4th, 2016, https://www.slashfilm.com/marvel-development-process/.

54.   Scott Huver, "The End of the Avengers."

55.   Joanna Robinson, "Secrets of the Marvel Universe."

56.   Peter Sciretta, "Your Marvel Phase 3 Questions."

57.   "Wall-E (2008)," IMDb Pro, accessed September 17, 2019, https://pro.imdb.com/title/tt0910970/details.

58.   "Up (2009)," IMDb Pro, accessed September 17, 2019, https://pro.imdb.com/title/tt1049413/details.

59.   "Toy Story 3 (2010)," IMDb Pro, accessed September 17, 2019, https://pro.imdb.com/title/tt0435761/details.

60.   Matt Wood, "How Has Marvel's Elimination of the Creative Committee Changed the MCU?" Cinema Blend, accessed September 13, 2019, https://www.cinemablend.com/news/2317962

/how-has-marvels-elimination-of-the-creative-committee-changed
-the-mcu.

61. Joanna Robinson, "Secrets of the Marvel Universe."

62. "Why Do the Avengers Fear this Man?"

63. Borys Kit and Kim Masters, "Marvel's Civil War: Why Kevin Feige Demanded Emancipation From CEO Ike Perlmutter," The Hollywood Reporter, September 3, 2015, https://www.hollywood reporter.com/heat-vision/marvels-civil-war-why-kevin-820147.

64. Borys Kit and Kim Masters.

65. Kim Masters and Matthew Belloni, "Marvel Shake-Up: Film Chief Kevin Feige Breaks Free of CEO Ike Perlmutter (Exclusive)," The Hollywood Reporter, August 31, 2015, https://www .hollywoodreporter.com/news/marvel-shake-up-film-chief -819205.

66. Nicole Laporte, "What You Need to Know About Marvel Entertainment's Mysterious Chairman—and Why Disney is Keeping Quiet," Fast Company, December 3, 2018, https://www.fast company.com/90273744/why-is-disney-mum-about-its-shadowy -marvel-entertainment-chairman.

Conclusion

1. "Spider-Man (2002)," IMDb Pro.

2. Ben Fritz, The Big Picture, 79.

3. "The Amazing Spider-Man 2 (2014)," IMDb Pro, accessed October 2, 2019, https://pro.imdb.com/title/tt1872181?rf=cons_tt _atf&ref_=cons_tt_atf.

4. Ben Fritz, *The Big Picture*, 113.

5. Ben Fritz, 234.

6. Ryan Faughnder, "Inside the deal that brought Sony's 'Spider-Man' back to Marvel's cinematic universe," *Los Angeles Times*, June 26, 2017, https://www.webcitation.org/6w3HBw0VI?url =http://www.latimes.com/business/hollywood/la-fi-ct-sony -marvel-spider-man-20170626-story.html. Archived from the original on December 28, 2017, retrieved September 12, 2019, http://www.latimes.com/business/hollywood/la-fi-ct-sony -marvel-spider-man-20170626-story.html.

7. Joel Meares, "Kevin Feige's Oral History."

8. Scott Huver, "The End of the Avengers."

9. Spencer Harrison, Arne Carlsen, and Hiha Škerlavaj, "Marvel's Blockbuster Machine," *Harvard Business Review,* July–August 2019, https://hbr.org/2019/07/marvels-blockbuster-machine.

10. Haleigh Foutch, "What It Takes."

11. Joel Meares, "Kevin Feige's Oral History."

12. Nicholas Mojica, "Marvel and Fox Traded 'Guardians of the Galaxy 2' and 'Deadpool' Characters," International Business Times, November 16, 2016, https://www.ibtimes.com/marvel -fox-traded-guardians-galaxy-2-deadpool-characters-2447099.

13. Anthony Breznican, "Will the Marvel Cinematic Universe ever . . . end?" *Entertainment Weekly,* April 15, 2016, https://ew.com/article /2016/04/15/will-marvel-cinematic-universe-ever-end/.

14. Joel Meares, "Kevin Feige's Oral History."

15. Peter Sciretta, "Kevin Feige on 'Doctor Strange.'"

16. Yasmin Vought, "Why Doctor Strange Almost Cost Scott Derrickson Everything," Yahoo! Lifestyle, October 18, 2016, https:// au.lifestyle.yahoo.com/scott-derrickson-spent-an-obscene -amount-money-to-land-doctor-strange-32935226.html.

17. Joanna Robinson, "Secrets of the Marvel Universe."

18. Taryn Finley, "Here Are the Black People Behind the Scenes who Made 'Black Panther' a Reality," Huffpost, February 15, 2018, https://www.huffpost.com/entry/here-are-the-black -people-behind-the-scenes-who-made-black-panther-a-reality _n_5a80de55e4b08dfc9305611c.

19. "Black Panther," Rotten Tomatoes, accessed September 18, 2019, https://www.rottentomatoes.com/m/black_panther_2018.

20. Joel Meares, "Kevin Feige's Oral History."

21. Gavia Baker-Whitelaw, et al, "Your complete guide to the Marvel Cinematic Universe," The Daily Dot, July, 2019, https://www .dailydot.com/parsec/mcu-movies-order-marvel-cinematic -universe-timeline/.

22. "Captain Marvel (2019)," IMDb Pro, accessed September 20, 2019, https://pro.imdb.com/title/tt4154664/filmmakers.

23. Joel Meares, "Kevin Feige's Oral History."

24. "Captain Marvel (2019)," IMDb Pro.

25. Joel Meares, "Kevin Feige's Oral History."

26. Scott Huver, "The End of the Avengers."

27. Scott Huver.

28. Kirsten Acuna, "19 Photos that Show how 'Averngers: Infinity War' Looks Without Visual Effects," Insider, April 16, 2019, https://www.insider.com/avengers-infinity-war-without-special-effects-2018-8.

29. Graeme McMillan, "'Avengers 4' Runtime is Currently 3 Hours," *Hollywood Reporter*, November 8, 2018, https://www.hollywood reporter.com/heat-vision/avengers-4-runtime-is-3-hours-making-it-longest-marvel-movie-ever-1159618.

30. *Marvel Studios: The First Ten Years*, 110.

31. *Marvel Studios: The First Ten Years*, 116.

32. Joanna Robinson, "Secrets of the Marvel Universe."

33. Sarah Whitten, "Disney Bought Marvel for $4 billion in 2009, a Decade Later It's Made More that $18 billion at the Global Box Office, CNBC, July 21, 2019, https://www.cnbc.com/2019/07/21/disney-has-made-more-than-18-billion-from-marvel-films-since-2012.html.

34. Jennifer M. Wood, "10 Highest-Grossing Movie Franchises of All Time," Mental Floss, March 18, 2019, http://mentalfloss.com/article/70920/10-highest-grossing-movie-franchises-all-time.

35. Eric Goldman, "The Winder Soldier."

36. "Disney and 21st Century Fox Announce per Share Value in Connection with $71 Billion Acquisition," The Walt Disney Company, March 19, 2019, https://www.thewaltdisneycompany.com/disney-and-21st-century-fox-announce-per-share-value-in-connection-with-71-billion-acquisition.

37. "The Walt Disney Company To Acquire Twenty-First Century Fox, Inc., After Spinoff Of Certain Businesses, For $52.4 Billion In Stock," The Walt Disney Company, December 14, 2017, https://www.thewaltdisneycompany.com/walt-disney-company-acquire-twenty-first-century-fox-inc-spinoff-certain-businesses-52-4-billion-stock-2/.

38. Josh Rottenberg, "What Disney's Acquisition of Fox Could Mean for Marvel's Superheroes," *Los Angeles Times*, March 8, 2019, https://www.latimes.com/entertainment/movies/la-et-mn-disney-fox-merger-marvel-superheroes-kevin-feige-20190308-story.html.

39. Meg James, "Disney Says Fox Purchase to be Final by March 20," Lost Angeles Times, March 12, 2019, https://www.latimes.com/ business/hollywood/la-fi-ct-disney-fox-deal-march-20-20190312 -story.html.

40. Rachel Yang, "Sony 'Disappointed' Marvel Boss Kevin Feige Won't Be Part of Next Spider-Man Movie," *Entertainment Weekly*, August 21, 2019, https://ew.com/movies/2019/08/21/sony -disappointed-marvel-boss-kevin-feige-wont-be-part-future -spider-man-movies.

41. Mark Hughes, "How the Marvel-Sony 'Spider-Man' Dispute Will Be Solved One Way or Another [Updated]," *Forbes*, August 21, 2019, https://www.forbes.com/sites/markhughes/2019/08/21 /how-the-marvel-sony-spider-man-dispute-will-be-solved-one -way-or-another/#43dcf8f46b50.

42. "Marvel Studios," IMDb Pro, accessed September 20, 2019, https://pro.imdb.com/company/co0051941/?ref_=tt_co_prod _co.

43. Spencer Harrison, Arne Carlsen, and Hiha Škerlavaj, "Marvel's Blockbuster Machine."

44. Joanna Robinson, "Secrets of the Marvel Universe."

45. Scott Huver, "The End of the Avengers."

INDEX

HarperCollins
Leadership
An Imprint of HarperCollins

THE
NBA
STORY

Available now from HarperCollins Leadership

CHAPTER ONE

THE FOUNDING AND STARTUP YEARS

The fast-paced excitement of today's NBA, with mega popular multimillion-dollar athletes and a multibillion-dollar television deal, started out, like most businesses, on a wing and a prayer. The hope was that such a competitive sport could bring some excitement and joy to a nation that had just played an integral part in World War II. Soldiers were back home, families were moving to the suburbs, and the time was right to grow a professional indoor, winter sports league that would not conflict with the nation's beloved summer pastime, baseball. It was a sport that had grown organically, starting as a game played in school gymnasiums, playgrounds, and YMCAs, then graduated to high school and college teams. It had already gone professional, but the NBA was going to improve upon the business of basketball as never seen before.

The National Basketball Association was the result of a business merger. It took place initially in 1946 when two rival men's basketball leagues, both struggling for different reasons, merged, the National Basketball League (NBL) and the Basketball Association of America (BAA). Together they remained a larger version of the BAA for three seasons before being officially billed as the National Basketball Association (NBA) in 1949. However, NBA statistics include those final three BAA seasons and the 1946 merger is widely considered the league's starting point.

Unlike many businesses, the NBA was conceived as, and remains, an entirely independent and fully self-managed organizational body (a limited corporation) whose members, the teams, are franchises operating as businesses that are independently owned. In 1946, each team paid a franchise fee of $10,000. Today, a new team entering the NBA would pay upward of $300 million.

The league operated, and continues to operate, under a constitution and a set of bylaws that constitute a contract among the members of the association, who are the owners, now sometimes referred to as governors. These team owners worked out the details of the league constitution and bylaws. The NBA Constitution spells out the governance structure of the league, including the rights and responsibilities of the team owners, the board of governors, and the commissioner. The NBA bylaws provide the framework for the operation of the league, which includes team and player requirements.

The league commissioner, known as the league president until 1967, would be elected by the owners. He was granted disciplinary power, dispute resolution authority, and decision-making authority, including the power to appoint other officers and committees. The owners, in conjunction with the initial league president, created the initial league rules, which were based, to a large degree, on the rules of the previous leagues and on those used in college basketball. It should also be noted that in the initial season, the NBA had a salary cap, which was eliminated after just one season and did not return for nearly forty years.

While the league was now in the startup phase, funded almost entirely by the franchise owners, issues arose almost immediately, which is not unusual following such a merger. The most notable concern was that while the leagues both offered the same product, professional men's basketball, they had radically different markets: small town and big city.

The National Basketball League, established in 1937, consisted primarily of Midwestern teams sponsored by some of the major corporations of the time, such as the Anderson Packers founded by the owners of a meat packing business in Anderson, Indiana, and the Akron Firestone Non-Skids, named for the Firestone Tire and Rubber Company, based in Akron, Ohio. The NBL teams played most of their games for small crowds in small venues. The Indianapolis Olympians, for example, played in the Hinkle Fieldhouse while the Fort Wayne Pistons actually played their home games in the North Side High School gymnasium. Five of the teams in the current NBA trace their roots back to the NBL. What made the NBL worthy of the merger was that they had the more talented, better-known collegiate players, and college basketball had already gained notoriety with tournaments dating back to the 1920s.

Meanwhile, the Basketball Association of America featured teams in larger markets, which played at venues such as at Madison Square Garden, home to the New York Knicks, and the Boston Garden, home to the Celtics. The big markets were a plus, especially when it came to local marketing, at the expense of the teams, and drawing larger crowds, However, the caliber of play was not at the level of the NBL teams.

The plan was to have four of the more successful NBL franchises join the BAA to complete the merger and hopefully bring together the star players from smaller markets with the drawing power of the teams playing in major markets. This would mean people in New York City or Boston, for example, could see top young stars, (still well-known from their college days), even if they were not on the home teams.

Launching the Business

The new league unveiled their product in Canada on November 1, 1946. While the league was still technically the BAA, this is considered the first-ever NBA game and it was played between the New York Knicks and the Toronto Huskies in front of a crowd of 7,090 at Maple Leaf Garden. It was not a bad turnout considering Toronto was known as a "hockey town." Even the arena, Maple Leaf Arena, was named for the city's NHL team. Longtime sportswriter Sam Goldaper, covering the game, wrote that the game "bore little resemblance to the leaping, balletic version of today's NBA. That game was from a different era of low-scoring basketball, a time when hoops as a pro spectacle was just coming out of the dance halls. Players did not routinely double-pump or slam-dunk. The fact of the matter was that the players did not and could not jump very well. Nor was there a 24-second clock; teams had unlimited time to shoot. The jump shot was a radical notion, and those who took it defied the belief of many coaches that nothing but trouble occurred when a player left his feet for a shot."[1] The Knicks won the league opener 68–66.

Maurice Podoloff

The person responsible for bringing the two leagues together was Maurice Podoloff, a distinguished attorney who headed the BAA from its inception. Podoloff was also president of the American Hockey League and founder of the New Haven Arena which he opened in the mid-1920s with his brothers. He was more knowledgeable in law and real estate than he was in sports. However, being a good negotiator served him well while dealing with the differing personalities of the team owners. Following the merger, Podoloff would serve as president of the new league which would include seventeen teams in three divisions. The season would run from October through March with each team having an awkward schedule which had teams playing between sixty-two and sixty-eight games, followed by playoffs in April.

Podoloff would spend seventeen years at the helm of the NBA, constantly supporting team owners in their quest to stay financially solvent. He introduced the college draft in 1947 which would bring new talent into the league every year and secured the league's first television deals for the NBA, first in 1953 with the DuMont Network for one season and then a long-term deal starting in 1954 with NBC.

Startup Years

Since the NBA was not a totally new business, it had an established product with professional men's basketball, there was already a small but steady fan base. The franchises maintained most of their players, some of whom had already developed a local following. League offices were maintained by a small staff in New York City while the owners maintained their franchise offices and remained enthusiastic during the early years, well-aware that they still held the purse strings, and that if their enthusiasm weaned they could exchanges players, sell the team, look to relocate or dissolve the franchise entirely.

College basketball provided the most significant competition to the league in the early years. However, the popularity of the college game also worked in favor of the league by providing talent once Podoloff initiated the college draft. This attracted fans who had read about college stars to see if they were as good as the rave reviews in the sports pages.

Among the NBA players who were already well known from their college days and had established themselves as stars in their local markets were Dolph Schayes, Neil Johnston, Bob Pettit, and Paul Arizin. While they all excelled in the early years of the league, one additional player was noteworthy for his impact on the sport and that was George Mikan. He played for the BAA, and then the NBA, for the Minneapolis Lakers. Mikan was the NBA's first big man, at 6'10", 245 pounds, and the first *must-see* superstar. He not only led his team to five titles, but he drew fans wherever the Lakers played. Mikan also created the drill for big men to practice shooting (known as the Mikan Drill) and was the impetus for several of the league's rule changes.

Despite the presence of Mikan and a favorable environment for the league, overall ticket sales remained low, particularly in the small markets, and there were no major television deals to drive revenue and promote the league during those first few seasons. In fact, college doubleheaders were still bigger draws than NBA games. Several NBA teams had difficulty scheduling their home games around ice hockey, boxing, and other events at some of the major arenas.

The league was almost entirely dependent on ticket sales as a source of revenue and Podoloff, along with the team owners, were constantly trying to market the product. To help publicize the new league, Podoloff hired J. Walter Kennedy, who was well known within the sports media establishment, having served as the publicity director for the Harlem Globetrotters on their national and international tours.

Movement and Contraction

In hopes of increasing attendance, several team owners moved their franchises to new markets, some making several moves before finding a more permanent home. Teams such as the Tri-City Blackhawks would move to Milwaukee in 1951 in hopes of gaining more attendance. When that didn't happen, they moved to St. Louis in 1955 where they would play for thirteen years before moving to Atlanta, where they remain today. The Fort Wayne Pistons would leave the high school gymnasium for an arena in Detroit in 1957; they too have stayed put. Other teams would move to larger markets, where they would either thrive or move again, such as the Rochester Royals who, due to lack of profitability, started making their way across the country, first to Cincinnati, then to Kansas City-Omaha and finally to Sacramento, where they were anointed "Kings."

In some cases, owners found a new market that was eager to watch professional basketball, so they moved their teams, while in other cases, owners failed miserably. Several disgruntled team owners tried to move their teams, but could not secure a profitable city with an arena in which to play. It was (and still is) also quite difficult to sell a franchise in a fledgling young business. As a result, some team owners threw in the towel early on, deciding that it was better to take smaller losses rather than hanging onto a sinking ship in a struggling league. Contraction within the NBA dropped the league from the original seventeen teams down to ten by the second season (eleven with the addition of the Baltimore Bullets). The league was down to just eight teams by the start of the 1955–56 season. It wouldn't be until 1970, some twenty-one years later, that the NBA would return to the seventeen-team league at which they started.

Innovation Saves the NBA

Maurice Podoloff, an astute businessman, provided the league with a strong business plan, built in part on the wisdom of notable management consultant Peter Drucker, who emphasized the need to recognize what the customer wants. In this case, the customers were the fans, and they wanted to see a fast-paced game between some of the country's finest athletes. With that in mind, Podoloff was still looking for suggestions to improve the fan experience.

Led by George Mikan, the new league was generating fan interest, as anticipated, plus the NBA was drawing additional crowds in the early years by having the Harlem Globetrotters as an opening act, largely thanks to J. Walter Kennedy. The Globetrotters, formed in 1926, were established worldwide as entertainers who would bring their remarkable mixed bag of basketball skills and comedic repartee to the court in a preliminary game before the NBA teams would tip-off. They were crowd-pleasers wherever they went, and the NBA was glad to have them bring more ticket holders into the arenas.

It's also worth mentioning that in 1950 two of the Globetrotters, Chuck Cooper Lloyd and Nathaniel "Sweetwater" Clifton, along with West Virginia State University star, Earl Lloyd, became the first three African Americans to play in the young league. Cooper debuted for the Celtics, Clifton for the Knicks, and Lloyd for the Washington Capitals.

Yet the league still wasn't making money. The biggest problem the new league faced went beyond the location of franchises or scheduling home games in the major arenas. It also went beyond any competition from other sports. The league's problems were internal. The NBA was a new business without an exciting product. The games had become methodical and fans were simply bored. The lack of scoring was a huge problem. Teams would get a lead and then stall, holding onto the ball, killing as much time as they could while sending fans into a stupor. The only ways to get the ball back was for a player to foul someone on the opposing team and after they made free throws they would get possession, or they would need to get a rebound off a missed free throw. This resulted in turning the game into tedious free throw shooting contests.

In 1950, the league hit rock bottom when Fort Wayne defeated Minnesota in the lowest-scoring game in NBA history. The game, called the Fort Wayne Freeze by Eric Nadel (ironically) in his book called *The Night Wilt Scored 100: Tales from Basketball's Past*, was a situation in which the Fort Wayne Pistons were in Minneapolis to play the Lakers, who sported the league's brightest star George Mikan, and a twenty-nine-game winning streak. The Pistons had a plan, which was simply to stall by holding onto the basketball as long as possible. Writes Nadel, "The referees could do nothing to speed up the game and the fans were irate when the first half ended—even though the Lakers held a 13–11 lead. The Piston players had to surround their coach, Murray Mendenhall, from outraged fans on the way to the locker room." When the game ended with the Pistons winning by the score of 19–18, "Podoloff instructed the owners and coaches never to let that happen again," wrote Nadel.[2]

Innovation was sorely needed; clearly something had to be done to speed up the game. In 1954, with the game desperately in need of a shot in the arm the owner of the Syracuse Nationals, Danny Biasone, and his general manager, Leo Ferris, came up with an idea. A team in possession of the ball would have only 24 seconds in which to take a shot, otherwise the ball would be turned over to the other team. The owners voted in favor of utilizing what would be called the 24-second clock. Rarely does a rule change, or changing a product, show immediate results, but in this case, it made a world of difference. The first game played with the 24-second clock finished with a score of 98–95. The pace of the game changed significantly, and the fans loved it. Suddenly there was a quickness and an urgency to score. Players were running up court, throwing the ball around and no longer taking forever to take a shot. In short, NBA basketball as we know it today was born in 1954, and fans saw a radical difference in the sport. This one simple rule change initiated by Biasone and Ferris did nothing less than save the NBA.

Improvements

Like any forward-thinking business, the NBA looked at the trends established in the league and made changes to encourage or discourage what they felt would help improve the game draw of fans. Along with the 24-second clock, the NBA made a number of improvements to their product during the early years in the form of rule changes, some of which were initiated by the league's star player who used his size to, unintentionally, influence such adjustments. For example, the foul lanes were widened from six to twelve feet for the 1954–55 season, primarily because George Mikan could reach out and grab a missed free throw and simply put it in the basket. Mikan could also stand in front of the basket and swat away anything that appeared to be going in.

As a result of Mikan, the goal-tending role, which had been initiated in the National Collegiate Athletic Association (NCAA) a few years earlier, was also adopted by the NBL and then by the NBA. Clearly all new businesses need to adjust as they move forward and the NBA adjusted their product as necessary.

The Players' Union

While the league suddenly had greater hope for survival with the introduction of the 24-second clock, and other new rules, the players had a number of off-court concerns.

According to NBA history, players had no per diem, no minimum wage, no health benefits, no pension plan, and the average player salary was roughly $8,000 in the early 1950s. Issues such as transportation from city to city were often challenging and players were frequently on their own when it came to getting a bus or train to the next game.[3]

The NBA players loved the game but were clearly, and vocally, frustrated by the league's inability to provide benefits. In 1954–55 season, with the league still in the formative years, and job security depending on the stability of each team, Bob Cousy (of the Boston Celtics) one of the league's premier players, decided it was time to unionize the players. Cousy knew he would need the support of other prominent players if he was

going to make his plan work, so he reached out to the highest
profile talent on other teams, such as Carl Braun of the New
York Knicks, Dolph Schayes of the Syracuse Nationals, and Paul
Arizin of the Philadelphia Warriors to help drum-up player support for the union. The plan worked and the National Basketball Players Association (NBPA) was formed. It was the first
players' union in organized sports in the United States.[4]

After gathering several grievances of the players, Cousy took
the list of concerns to Podoloff, who now officially served as
league's first commissioner. Along with the team owners, Podoloff put off the NBPA concerns for nearly two years until
Cousy sought out a possible union affiliation with the AFL-CIO.
This got Podoloff's attention, yet it still took some time before
the league acted. Finally, several of the early player concerns
were agreed upon by the owners and the players' union in 1957
including a seven dollar per diem, other reasonable traveling
expenses, an increase in the playoff pool, and reasonable moving expenses for players traded during a season. Although the
NBPA was making some headway, it would take several years
before the owners began taking the union seriously. Frustrated
by the owners' attitudes toward the union, Cousy turned the
reins over to his Boston teammate Tom Heinsohn, who took on
the issue of a player's pension, and also ran up against resistance from the owners.[5]

As the league was perched to move into the 1960s, players'
grievances would continue to be a sticking point for owners.
Yet, the league, after a long fourteen-year gestation period, was
finally seeing the ascent they had hoped for, and some teams
were now making money.

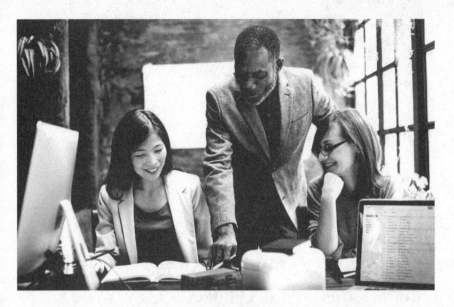

The future is within reach.

When you start making your goals a top priority, everything falls into place. Learn from the leaders inspiring millions & apply their strategies to your professional journey.

Leadership Essentials Blog

Activate 180 Podcast

Interactive E-courses

Free templates

LEADERSHIP
ESSENTIALS
by HarperCollins Leadership

For more business and leadership advice and resources, visit hcleadershipessentials.com.

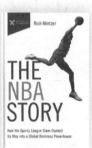